Changing the World

VINCENT COSMAO

Changing the World

An Agenda for the Churches

TRANSLATED FROM THE FRENCH BY JOHN DRURY

ORBIS BOOKS
Maryknoll, New York 10545

The Catholic Foreign Mission Society of America (Maryknoll) recruits and trains people for overseas missionary service. Through Orbis Books Maryknoll aims to foster the international dialogue that is essential to mission. The books published, however, reflect the opinions of their authors and are not meant to represent the official position of the society.

Bible quotations are from the Revised Standard Version, Oxford Annotated Edition.

First published as *Changer le monde: Une tâche pour l'Eglise,* copyright © 1979 Les Editions du Cerf, 29, bd Latour-Maubourg, Paris

English translation copyright © 1984 Orbis Books, Maryknoll, NY 10545

Manufactured in the United States of America

Manuscript Editor: William E. Jerman

Library of Congress Cataloging in Publication Data

Cosmao, Vincent.
  Changing the world.

  Translation of: Changer le monde.
  1. Sociology, Christian (Catholic) 2. Church and the world. I. Title.
  BX1753.C6313   1984   261.1   84-5153
  ISBN 0-88344-107-1 (pbk.)

Contents

Preface to the English Translation

When I wrote this book, in the late 1970s, I was trying to do two things:
(1) recapitulate a stream of reflection then in progress on development;
(2) lay the groundwork for a theological development whose axis would be
a rereading of God's word vis-à-vis questions raised by the problematic of
development as vital for understanding the faith and translating it into
action—for taking full practical and theoretical account of one's relationship to God in accordance with the preaching and practice of Jesus.

At that time, the prospective of the establishment of a New International
Economic Order, opened up by the Declaration of the Sixth Extraordinary
General Assembly of the United Nations Organization, on May 1, 1974,
had not yet been dimmed, as it has since. It was still possible to hope that
this might yield a framework for a better understanding of underdevelopment, and for the exploration of paths that would lead to the broadening of
development.

Today the data of the problem have been profoundly modified—partly,
indeed, in virtue of the reactions of industrialized countries to the conflicts
over oil that have permitted the Third World, by lining up behind the OPEC
countries, to pose this problem in terms which meant that a politically negotiated solution might be found. It seemed that it might be possible to transform the system of international trade within which, until that time, the
countries that were only sellers of primary products had to pay the costs.
Their unilateral, "arbitrary" increase in oil prices exposed the "constructed," artificial, imposed nature of the prevailing system of international exchange. Finding themselves, in turn, dependent, the industrialized
nations were willing to consider negotiating the conditions of their dependence, in the collective administration of a generalized interdependence.

One could see that this "state of grace" would not be of long duration,
and it was not. Today other sources of energy are being turned to. Economists and others who still continue to speak of an economy based on expen-
sive energy are doing so out of acquired habit rather than familiarity with
the real world. It is no longer upon energy, but upon information, and its
transmission or manipulation by integrated circuits, that economic progress
and the reorganization of societies now depend. Underdeveloped countries
find themselves once more in the situation in which they were before the
"oil war"—dependent on imported technology imposed on them and ever
thereafter needful to them—without any favorable repercussion on the
prices fixed for their products, when they find a market for them. They are
more and more dependent on the industrialized countries for the most indis-

pensable primary products, those necessary for their very subsistence. In addition, their accumulated debt and their food needs—neither problem a soluble one—create a new interdependence. Creditors and grain speculators are most anxious to keep the system going, for they would be the first to lose out if it ran into difficulties.

But while negotiations—whose possibility, indeed whose necessity, had been recognized so recently—marked time, practically everywhere in the Third World a process of development appeared, characterized by the launching of the self-determination of peoples via their conscientization, their self-organization, and their will to assign highest priority to their most elementary—alimentary—self-sufficiency. In other words, their first aim was the satisfaction of their own essential needs—the objective assigned to the New International Economic Order. The goal of self-sufficiency might demand an interruption in production for the world market for a time. But it had to include—via the resuscitation or promotion of the collective subject, the only possible agent of its own development—the basis for a more global development. And the dynamic of global development, in confrontation with the rigidities of the prevailing system, would pose the political question all over again—the question of societal transformation. The heightened consciousness and enhanced organization of societies beginning to develop will perhaps replace oil as the driving power for the construction of a world society, a global society embracing all human groups.

Decades of reflection on development had demonstrated that it was the social and cultural nature of problems that was crucial. And yet these problems had so long been posed in economic terms alone. An underdeveloped society suffers more radically from destructuration than from the technological lag. The mechanisms of its relationships—exchange of goods, services, information—which permitted it to "function" as a society, become disarticulated. Extraverted, dependent, it sees its constitutive subgroupings articulate themselves helter-skelter amid the societal order on which it depends for the essential element of its activities. Dispossessed of the management of its own dynamic, it is satellitized, and thereby it disintegrates. Its potential for regaining control of itself, and again becoming the agent of its own development, in a process analogous to a resurrection, confirms this analysis. And it leads to the prioritization of the cultural and spiritual factors of social dynamics, along with an international political approach. For better or for worse, the experience of recent years evinces the resurgence of hidden springs of social vitality.

Reflection on development thus grows richer, even as its practice seems stymied, and the theological approach that I have sketched in this book still seems pertinent and promising to me. The central problem is that of the articulations, or mediations, that will permit the passage from reflection on development to a rereading of the word of God.

The concept of sin, reduced to its simplest expression—contradiction of God—can be used to analyze our world. From being a world that produces spheres of underdevelopment and absolute poverty, a "world of sin," it must be converted, liberated, in order to become, by collective endeavor, a world less faulty, where a global community of goods may become reality (chap. 7).

The other articulation upon which this book hinges (chap. 3) is that of bringing to light the "laws" of structuration, in inequality, of societies left to their own inertia, and the "laws" of the sacralization of social organizations, a sacralization that is all the mightier for the fact that societies are becoming still more inegalitarian.

Swimming against the tide of this inertia, this entropy, the Judeo-Christian tradition appears to be buoyed up by a will to actively resist what happens in societies when they fail to organize themselves to provide at least this: that no one be in need. The rereading of the word of God is very provocative here in that it makes no appeal to a utopia, not even a messianic one, but only to a practice, to be taken up ever and again, for which no model is furnished, but only the criterion of what is unacceptable: that someone lacks something necessary (Matt. 25). To keep things from being this way, the political restructuration of society becomes a task in which the church, in its own way, must take its part. One need only reread the Bible and the history of the church with this thought in mind and there will be no end to the discovery of peaks and abysses in society, including outright perversions, when God is "used" to gain unquestioning acceptance of a social organization in which the poor—Christ—are hungry, naked, strangers, imprisoned.

There is another articulation to be explored. It is suggested by the very mystery of Easter. Underdevelopment leads to death, whereas God raises to life. The poor, who arise and walk in response to God's call, are actualizing, in their practice, the action of the Spirit who raises the dead. It is clear, then, that God is at work today. Those who undertake to create the conditions needed so that all may have life proclaim this in a living faith, whose sign of authenticity is that it vanquishes the fear of death.

Reflection along these lines, of which my effort represents one moment, is moving ahead, then, and delving deeper into an understanding of the dramatic problems of our times—and into an understanding of the word of God in relation to the reality for whose transformation it calls, in order that human beings, alive with God's life, may manifest God's glory.

Foreword

Development: A Task for the Church

"Changing the world" was one of the phrases that Father L.-J. Lebret liked to use to dramatize the scale of the multi-faceted struggle for development that had become the axis of his life as dedicated theoretician and practitioner of developmental planning and as a man of God. Like the prophets, he publicized the catastrophes he saw embedded in the contradictions of international life. But he also proposed ways to deal with those contradictions and to effect the changes required in relationships between nations and social groups. As time went on, those needed transformations took on for him the dimensions of a worldwide revolution.

A few weeks before his death in 1966, Father Lebret was still hunting for a title for the book he was writing for development proponents. He wanted a title that would sum up the tasks at hand. He finally settled on the phrase *développement=révolution solidaire:* "development=revolution in solidarity." Thus he related revolution to the achievement of solidarity, while suggesting that there could be no real solidarity without revolution.

"Changing the world" was the task he labored at all his life: with deep-sea fishermen, with pioneers in land management, with Third World leaders who tried to implement development policies, and with officials of international organizations. Father Lebret had also spent his whole life trying to alert Christians to the worldwide misery for which they had to shoulder responsibility. In his eyes the wounded man on the road to Jericho had come to symbolize humanity waiting for a good Samaritan as priests and Levites continued to pass by. Father Lebret was so deeply conscious of those urgent needs and tasks that any expenditure of energy that disregarded them struck him as "insane."

As Vatican II drew to a close, the task of mobilizing the Catholic Church for the transformation of the world became one of his priorities. Contemplative that he was, he knew how to lose himself in God through abandonment of self. But he was no less certain that the "journey to God" takes the road of "action." He thought that the audience at the church's disposal should be placed in the service of development—which is to say, committed to the task of reorganizing the world.

The inspiration that motivated him can be found in Paul VI's encyclical on socio-political development, *Populorum Progressio* (1967). Father Lebret was the chief motivating force behind that encyclical. Despite its understandable reserve concerning "revolutionary uprisings," for which it nevertheless leaves room as in extreme cases (n. 31), the encyclical goes on to say: "continuing development calls for bold innovations that will work profound changes. The critical state of affairs must be corrected for the better without delay" (n. 32). It calls for a reorganization of international relationships, urging Christians to ponder and live their faith in terms of a collective task: reconstructing the world. It was a summons to action based upon Christian participation in the resurrection of Christ and the creation of the world.

Populorum Progressio spoke to a church already sensitized to developmental problems. It gave backing and encouragement to activist practices that were already in the process of shifting from palliative charitable activity to political action aimed at transforming the whole international system. Nevertheless the encyclical did not have the mobilizing impact that many would have.

Populorum Progressio was the culmination of an ecclesial initiative centered around "presence in the world" and stemming from the concepts of "social Catholicism" and "mission." It was promulgated at a time when movement was evident in church structures. But that very movement highlighted the crisis in the Catholic Church and the need for inner reconstruction by a "return to the sources"—the other main thrust of Vatican II. While the church continued to encourage lay persons to assume their responsibilities in society and international life, stress was increasingly placed on the "specific mission" of the church "to proclaim the gospel message," as if to suggest that there was a contradiction between transforming the world and making God known through the spread of the gospel.

The document of the 1971 Synod of Bishops, *Justice in the World*, expressly states: "Action on behalf of justice and participation in the transformation of the world fully appear to us as a constitutive dimension of the preaching of the gospel . . . of the church's mission for the redemption of the human race and its liberation from every oppressive situation" (n. 6). But this statement was then to be subjected to a processs of "clarification," which some saw as an effort to reassure those who were disturbed to see the subversive power of the gospel message brought out in the open.

Close observation and analysis do suggest, however, that there was a certain thrust in church life during this period. Its two high points in the Catholic Church were the 1967 encyclical and the 1971 Synod of Bishops—both during the papacy of Paul VI. They gave rise to a current in ecclesial life; its effects are visible today in the church's involvement in international life. That current could have become a theological current as well, if the political praxis of involved Christians had been understood as a praxis of the faith.

In 1967 I ventured to suggest that *Populorum Progressio* was calling for a "theology of development." By this term I did not mean a theological treatment of development based on the logic of the church's social teaching. I meant an interpretation of the life of faith based on its embodiment in development praxis. My suggestion was not really picked up.

Around the same time, however, a "theology of liberation" arose in Latin America. It did not stem from the encyclical. It stemmed from a process of generalization based on the analysis of underdevelopment in terms of dependence and on the involvement of Christians in liberation movements. European and North American Chistians working for development were also beginning to coordinate their activities and strategies in order to strike at the root causes of underdevelopment.

Thus churches in both highly industrialized and underdeveloped countries were mobilizing to participate effectively in the global effort to reorganize societies and their interrelationships. Worldwide networks of relationships were being established between activists—Christian or not—who were willing to be partners in the common struggle to change the world. But a discursive body of thought on this activity, one that would relate it to God in Jesus Christ, was not in evidence. Everywhere, to some extent, Christians who have invested their energy in this global effort still find themselves without a language in which to express their faith insofar as it is being lived in this particular way.

These Christians are fully conscious of the relevance of their activity and capable of accounting for it politically by an analysis of the mechanisms of underdevelopment. But they find it difficult to offer a theological account of it to other Christians or to church officials, even though they know from their own experience that in this work they are shaping and leading their lives under the eyes of God. Rebuffed as ideologues when they try to say who they really are—whether or not they call themselves revolutionaries, Marxists, or Christians for Socialism—they are regarded as deviants or dreamers. In some countries they are viewed as subversives and are persecuted for it. Elsewhere they are ignored by politicians or theoreticians who regard religion as incompatible with revolution.

In line with its original thrust, reflection on revolution has taken shape as a necessary protest against any and all sacralization of social organizations. Yet many find it hard to believe that such protest might also be lived out with reference to God, even when the experience of believers bears clear witness to that possibility.

In the comradeship of revolutionary movements, participants may come to recognize the authenticity of the commitment made by certain Christians. But that very fact raises doubts within the church about the compatibility of such a commitment and the faith. Efforts to formulate one's way of living such a commitment inevitably produce blunders and excesses. This only stiffens resistance within the church to efforts challenging the present organization of the world, which developed in close conjunction with the church's own expansion.

Ever since Europe, organized as Christendom, set out upon the conquest of the world, in the world internal transformations have involved a reaction against the church's centuries-long tutelage. Now that Europe itself is in the process of losing its central place, the church finds itself enmeshed in that decline. But the church remains unconsciously affected and guided by the certainties that took on shape and structure in the culture area that it controlled. Thus, in the church's eyes, "civilization" was equated with "Christian civilization." And although criticism of the negative effects of that civilization may be taken for granted today, it is much harder to recognize and admit that those effects followed almost of necessity from the dynamics of domination involved in the expansion of that civilization.

Ecclesial awareness continues to be shaped by the internal contradictions that have arisen in the church over the past two centuries. I refer to the impact of ideological confrontation with such things as the European revolutions, liberal democracies, various forms of socialism, and the achievements of science. To no small extent they help explain the church's incomprehension of praxis designed to "change the world" and its rejection of any line of reasoning that attempts to interpret that praxis as a praxis of the faith. The checkmating of all such efforts has long since become a well-rehearsed maneuver. One after another, the advocates of such efforts came to be regarded as lost to the church or lost to the cause of the effective transformation of social relationships.

There seems to be no place in the overall picture for a revolution that is lived in reference to God's design for the world.

On a global scale, however, the church does constitute a social and cultural space wherein unlike-minded persons might well meet. In that space representatives of underdeveloped countries who are seeking to regain control of their social dynamics and representatives of industrialized nations who are slow in taking cognizance of the rights of the poor have an opportunity to hear and understand each other. There they might be able to reach an agreement about the necessary and inevitable transformation in their present relationships. What they share in common would enable them to communicate with each other despite their disagreements.

Moreover, Third World exponents and development activists are gradually assuming their place in the church by modest efforts. Instead of trying to force their point of view, they may well achieve more by dedicating themselves as wholeheartedly as possible to that task of conscientization and the work of organizing and coordinating their collective efforts.

In their reflection on their praxis, these persons are calling for some "theological accompaniment." It is that call that has prompted me to write this book. Starting with an analysis of underdevelopment, I move on to a theological interpretation of the praxis to which such Christians have been led. My approach is to take issues one by one as they have come to be raised in de facto practice. Thus this theological effort links up with that of liberation theologians, even though reflection on development is its specific point of departure. My work is, I think, relevant and useful for those Christians who are trying to understand and explain the faith-rooted import of their committed efforts to transform the world.

Having tried out this material in study groups of all persuasions, I felt it was time to offer an overall presentation of a more detailed sort. But this work still represents a tentative, preliminary effort. Many of its component elements will have to be subjected to further scrutiny and argument.

Even in its present form, however, this work should be useful to those who are called to reflect theologically on their praxis. It is to them that my work is primarily addressed. It was their questions, as well as my own reading, that helped to shape my thoughts. And I have not considered it necessary to make reference to various texts that now and again enabled me to verify the pertinence of their questions.

My study is an ordered course of reflection. Thirty-three interconnected theses are presented in eight chapters. Each thesis is developed in a short section of its own. They may be read in isolation, but the essential context is provided by the entire work.

These pages were written during early-morning hours stolen from the business of day-to-day living. They lack the coherence and continuity that a work written on retreat or on a sabbatical might have had. But inasmuch as the issues are being raised afresh every day, I prefer to publish my remarks as they stand rather than wait for the leisure to rework them point by point. That might only tempt me to overformalize them.

The final pages were written just before the start of John Paul II's papacy. My feelings during those dramatic three hours only heightened my belief that the theses offered here deal with the basic set of problems facing the church in this new era of its life.

This work is dedicated principally to the memory of two persons: L.-J. Lebret (1897–1966), who wanted to "change the world"; and Paul VI (1897–1978), who took him seriously. When Paul VI sent me the text of *Populorum Progressio* in April 1967, he said, "This document is also a tribute to the memory of our beloved and respected and lamented Father Lebret."

Chapter 1

A New International Economic Order
and the Future of Humankind

During the five years from 1973 to 1979, the problem of voluntarily establishing a new international economic order was posed clearly, but the outlines of a solution were not worked out. It has become obvious that humanity will have to organize for the joint, collective conduct of its history. It will have to get used to taking the initiative in constructing the systems of relationships on which its collective life depends. And to do that, it will have to dismantle the systems of certainties, of things taken for granted as obvious and proven, that prompt it to regard such a task as useless or unthinkable. In short, humanity will have to ponder its future so that it can resolve to fashion that future.

Thesis 1: Before the end of this millennium, humanity will have to make a collective commitment to shaping a habitable earth.

In August 1978, the World Bank announced that at the end of this millennium 600 million men, women, and children would still be mired in "absolute poverty." It sounded the alarm—not for the first time—and furnished some data for sizing up this situation. On such acts of positive awareness will depend the very future of the human race.

A small and relatively decreasing minority of human beings will benefit from the unimaginable progress made possible by developments in the information sciences. There will be data networks handling information, computation, management, and various other services. At the same time, however, the ever-growing majority of human beings will find themselves in the grip of insoluble problems insofar as the satisfaction of their basic needs is concerned: food, clothing, housing. The total amount of land under cultivation for general consumption will shrink as more and more of it is monopolized for the production of goods wanted by the affluent. The same will apply to vegetal sources of energy, which will be more and more in demand by the affluent for transportation, temperature modification, and the maintenance of their mechanical or electronic robots.

Surrounded on all sides by famished, disinherited masses, the affluent minor-

1

ity will have to lock themselves up in their fortresses to escape the terrorist activities of desperate individuals and bands. Security will become an obsession, and the collective conscience will reconcile itself to the harsh measures needed to guarantee that security. Human rights, honed to a fine edge in definitions, will continue to be trampled underfoot—both by authorities entrusted with the maintenance of order and by those denouncing the established disorder.

From a human standpoint that is the scenario forced upon us when we contemplate the tendencies already germinal in reality. It is clear that contradictions between North and South are progressively taking the place of contradictions between East and West. The countries that were the first to embark on the process of industrialization will continue to advance, multiplying the production units of their multinational enterprises throughout the world. A few other countries endowed with rare or precious natural resources will gradually join in that process. For the rest of the world, however, the story will be different. The rural poor will have to scratch a meager living from their sterile lands, and the ever-growing number of unemployed in metropolitan areas will depend on food surpluses from the industrialized nations.

At some point, as the result of a poor harvest, the theoretical question of who gets into the lifeboat will turn into a concrete debate. Those who control the food supplies will decide who will be let on board and who will not. There will not be room for all, and some will be left in the surf to die of exhaustion.

Before humanity reaches that point, however, awareness of the drift of the situation will become widespread. Those destined to be victimized will be the first to become alarmed. Despair will give them the energy to make the necessary start, to take on the task of stopping and reversing the whole process. Awareness of the urgent issues will also come to the fore among some of the privileged, disinclined to enjoy affluence if the price is the annihilation of the masses.

Affluence itself is fragile, because technical progress can create more problems than it solves. The industrialized countries have already entered into crisis, and it will be solved only at the cost of various types of reorganization. That will entail new reshapings of societies and lifestyles. New opportunities will become available, but not for everyone. Humanity is in danger of becoming divided once again into two factions: a privileged elite of free human beings who can enjoy life, and a multitude of vassals or rejects left useless and unemployed.

Far from spreading automatically by virtue of its appeal, progress has a tendency toward concentration in the hands of those who possess the physical and intellectual capacities as well as the monetary resources needed to move into its sphere. Space travel, access to data banks, and personal use of available goods and information will not be within reach of the vast majority. Most will not have the slightest idea of how to take advantage of such things in order to gain admittance to the new lifestyle that will be the dominant model. In a "leisure civilization," where elective creativity will be the norm, the number of frustrated individuals will be beyond count. The visions already being hawked by advertising media relate only to the "idle rich" who are "cultivated" and "refined" enough to find their pleasure in such things.

Such is the new "continental drift" affecting all parts of the world. International "aid"—the transfer of capital resources, techniques, and know-how—cannot enable the underdeveloped countries to attain economic stability and eventually catch up with the industrialized nations (much less overtake them). Yet that was the dream that a wide-awake world deluded itself with for almost twenty years. The fact is that such aid only helps conceal what is really going on: the ever-increasing transfer of goods and work force from the periphery to the center, where the capabilities for research and innovation are concentrated.

In a world that lives on credit, where the indebtedness of the Third World amounts to about the same sum as the annual arms budget ($300 billion), the only needs that will be met will be those that can be solved by new possibilities (and hence new necessities) introduced by technology. After the automobile, the airplane, and household appliances, we shall see information and control media replacing means of transportation rendered obsolete by traffic congestion.

Elated by its creative power, which bears witness to the ability and vocation of humankind to create the conditions necessary for its existence by mastering nature, the modern world seems condemned to rush ahead pell-mell. But it is a mad race to the edge of an abyss—to the extent that the goods and services produced will necessarily be reserved for the few.

It is not the first time in history, of course, that the multitudes have been forced to look on while the "great ones" displayed their ostentation in their palaces, temples, and tombs. All that remains today of such ostentation are a few ruins and museum pieces for the most part. But today *is* the first time that humanity as a whole has been in a position to take conscious note of how misguided history is when it is steered by a few to ensure their maximum benefit and the misfortune of the majority. The means of destruction, now accumulated to the point of overkill, stand as a symbol of our present situation. The implementation of human ingenuity has now reached the point where the earth may become increasingly uninhabitable or even a desert waste. We admire the ruins of great civilizations that bear silent witness to human exploitation. But those civilizations now lie buried under forests or desert sands.

We must hope against hope that humanity will do something before it is too late. In its yearning for life it must find the inspiration it needs to envision and carry out the collective task it faces: the shaping of a habitable earth for all. When we contemplate bygone civilizations we cannot help but wonder about our present one, which continues to be built on the basis of inequalities. Is not such a civilization already undermined at its very foundations? Already doubts are creeping into our assumptions about its relevance and worth. Perhaps they are the first cracks through which the sands of the desert may filter. Perhaps they represent an opportunity to call things into question and thus begin the collective enterprise on which our future will depend. When it is no longer obvious which road to take, it becomes possible to try new paths.

Think of the brave deeds of human groups in the past. They have managed to survive on thankless lands and in harsh climates. Think of the thousands of years required to figure out the elementary actions and procedures that form the basis of agriculture, animal husbandry, and cooking. Why, then, should we despair of humanity's ability to pull itself together and confront the enormous challenge of the present age? Why can it not make the necessary shift to the collective organization of its life on this planet as a whole? The mastery of social dynamics is no more unthinkable than the mastery of nature. The shaping of a habitable earth for all will be the great challenge to be met by the end of this millennium.

It goes without saying that the de facto world—where humanity faces this task—is also the only possible place for comprehending and practicing faith in Jesus Christ. It is in history, taking shape step by step, that the church is built up. It is by participating in that history that the church is confronted with the real questions that give it access to what the word of God has to say.

These "worldly matters," on which depends the future of humanity, can no longer be shunted to the margin of ecclesial life. Their place is at the very heart of the church's practice of the faith. Taking due note of them will increasingly be seen as a necessity if the faith is to be taken seriously.

Growing in a world threatened with death, the church has a role to play in the salvage and reconstruction of that world. As we approach the end of the millennium in which Christianity has had a presence, we find the church being called back to its original truth and dynamism. In taking part in the task of organizing a world system in which all will have a chance to find fulfillment as human beings, the church is really being summoned to reconstruct itself and to carry out its mission. Perhaps the most significant sign of the times is this convergence of the necessities of human history with the main lines of sacred history.

Thesis 2: The decision and will to build a new system of relationships between nations and human groups has become a prerequisite for the continuation of human existence.

Societies are built upon the relationships established between human groups in the course of exchanging goods and services. The goods may be either material or symbolic; the exchanges constitute the very fabric of collective life.

These relationships have been structured and regulated over the course of centuries and millennia. In traditional societies it has been done by ongoing negotiation; in centralized societies those holding power have imposed laws. The characteristic feature of modern times is the confrontation between two working hypotheses or systems for regulating social relationships. One form of regulation is that based on market exchange, a type of negotiation. The other form is centralized or state planning. It is not too early to say that both systems, elaborated into theories, have revealed their limitations. In one way or another, they must complement and balance each other.

Whatever may come about at the level of states and national governments, the construction of a world society embracing all human groupings can come about only through negotiation. All nations must be willing to impose and accept certain constraints that will make their interchanges more effective and equitable. Inasmuch as no world authority exists as yet, the regulation of international relationships can come about only through joint construction of systems of obligations to which all are willing to submit.

It was that sort of negotiation that nonaligned and other Third World countries urged upon the industrialized nations when they called for the establishment of a new international economic order (declaration of the sixth extraordinary general assembly of the United Nations, May 1, 1974). For almost four years international discussion was polarized around that issue, though such negotiation never came about in fact. The resultant impasse can be only a temporary misfortune. Sooner or later this "impossible but necessary" task must be taken up again. The growing complexity of international relationships and international interdependence means that relationships between nations must be planned and organized. We must gradually fashion norms and structures that will regulate those relationships.

The norm of laissez-faire, based on the "natural" complementarity of "comparative advantages," has proved its ineffectiveness in promoting generalized progress. It leads inevitably to the domination of the weak by the strong, verifying Lacordaire's point on a world scale: in relationships between rich and poor, between strong and weak, it is freedom that oppresses and law that liberates. But before international relationships can be subjected to law, we must first draw up the law, article by article. And contrary to what one might be inclined to think, that task has already been addressed in large measure.

First, we have declarations, pacts, and conventions dealing with human rights, social freedoms, and social rights. They constitute the fragile but already defined basis of an international law that could provide the structure for the consensus needed to implement a collective project.

Secondly, we have the countless conventions and accords required to govern mail shipment, air and sea navigation, and the fight against diseases, pests, and pollution. They represent the first elements of international organization.

We have only begun our work, however. The whole complex of relationships between human groupings must be organized. We must create the systems of regulation we need to ensure their proper functioning in the general interest.

It is only natural that those enduring the consequences of the present "anarchy" are the ones calling for the construction of an order that might guarantee their legitimate rights. And it is also only natural that those benefiting from the norm of laissez-faire are not much inclined to submit to norms that would reduce their privileges.

But as interchanges grow more numerous and more complex, it will become increasingly evident that interests apparently opposed in the short run are actually complementary in the long run. The fact is that humanity is in communication with itself on the closed space of this planet. The coordination required upon the outbreak of an epidemic reveals that fact clearly. So do the worldwide repercussions of a bad harvest in the U.S.S.R., a drought in the African Sahel, or a frost in the coffee plantations of Brazil. All human beings clearly have an interest in the collective management of a patrimony that is not inexhaustible and that belongs to all by right.

The reluctance of the industrialized nations to participate in the joint planning being urged on them can readily be explained in terms of the tendency of the privileged to defend what they regard as hard-won rights. Nonetheless it bears witness to a disconcerting lack of vision over the long run and a failure to appreciate their own long-term interests. Protectionism—the logical result of refusing to take part in joint planning—leads inevitably to sclerosis. The narrow focusing of the industrialized nations on their own internal problems is one of the most disturbing symptoms of the world crisis. Even more disturbing, though quite understandable, is the growing self-centeredness of groups that regard themselves as pioneers in the effort at social progress.

Responsible employment promotion in the industrialized countries will presuppose that the dramatic underemployment in the Third World will be taken into account. From now on, economic and social problems, and hence political problems as well, cannot help but be world problems.

What representatives of the Third World proposed a few years ago was not a prefabricated model of an international order or a world plan. Instead they called for the start of an ongoing process of negotiation. All governments would participate in this process, whatever their economic or political strength might be, in order to bring about a redistribution of resources, production activities, and power. By jointly winning back control over their natural resources, particularly those that provide a basis for negotiation insofar as the industrialized countries need them (e.g., petroleum and phosphates), they were ensuring themselves the minimum of power needed to have some weight in the give and take of international exhange. This power play was enough to force recognition of the relevance of the negotiating process they were proposing. But it did not get the process going in earnest, and discussion remains stalled on such preliminary issues as the stabilization of prices for primary products and the renegotiation of Third World debts. We must get beyond the present impasse and resume a real process of negotiation, one aimed at establishing responsible management of humanity's common patrimony—that is, the earth it inhabits.

One threshold in human history was crossed with the shift from hunting and food-gathering to agriculture and stockbreeding. Now the day is coming when we shall have to shift from fishing to aquaculture and pisciculture. Otherwise the marine fauna that provides a part of our food supply will disappear.

Meanwhile, however, we must shift from "predatory hunting and gathering" insofar as the whole ensemble of available natural resources is concerned. Industrial economy has been organized around the assumption that raw materials and primary products have little or no value in themselves, that they acquire value only insofar as they are transformed into useful or necessary things. It is indeed true that petroleum is worthless so long as it lies buried underground. But once such resources are made available, and are depended on, and are not inexhaustible, we must manage them wisely. And we must look ahead to the replacements that will become necessary in the future, with all the changes they will occasion.

In shifting from hunting to stockbreeding, "primitive" humanity took charge of the reproduction of its food supplies. In shifting from the depredation of its primary resources to their careful management, modern humanity will take a step forward in mastering its relationship with nature. But it must still decide to take that step.

It is not just a matter of eliminating the vestiges of colonialism and "imperialism, the highest stage of capitalism." We must construct an economy and a set of social relationships effectively designed to transform the resources of our planet and to place them at the disposal of all who need them to organize and stabilize their life. Astonishing as it may seem to those who reason in terms of common sense, the fact is that we have not done so as yet. The exploitation of natural resources has become one of the means to power and wealth. It is not geared to the satisfaction of human needs. Consumption is determined by production, not vice versa. Production creates the need for its own products. When the vast majority lack the bare necessities of life, it is time to ponder and practice a redistribution of resources that will satisfy basic needs.

Come what may, the question of a new social, political, and economic order has been placed on the agenda. Moreover, the redeployment of production activities by multinational companies has produced, in the short run, increased unemployment in the industrialized countries. This has aroused public opinion in a way not seen before, when only the underdeveloped countries were feeling the consequences of uncontrolled industrialization. The effect of underdevelopment—namely, societal disintegration—is now making its way back to the industrialized population centers. This will accelerate awareness of the worldwide dimensions of the problem and of the need to organize on a worldwide scale in order to master it.

The peoples of the industrialized countries, on whom the reorganization of the world will depend in great part, will discover that they are the first who should be interested in the voluntary policy proposed to them by the Third World. The disintegration of a world united by colonialism has not eliminated relationships of interdependence. Formerly grounded on the basis of inequality, those relationships must now be made more equal through a cooperative effort. The voluntary policies required for the development of each country in isolation would be far more onerous than a coordinated effort designed to satisfy the needs of all.

Yet this obvious fact has not yet forced its way on the consciousness of human societies. Since the neolithic period they have tended to barricade themselves in their little corner of the earth. To cross the threshold before which humanity now finds itself, there must be a radical transformation of the mental structures formed over the long millennia when societies defended their own piece of territory because they were unable to organize for peaceful coexistence on a broader scale.

Thesis 3: The restructuring of international life entails the transformation of mental structures.

So long as the existing order of things, whatever it might be, is taken for granted by the vast majority of human beings or a given human grouping, transformation can come about only by force or by the persevering work of an activist minority whose convictions overturn accepted ideas. The great mutations in human history have been effected by minorities sure enough of their truth and their power to impose their viewpoints on humanity in the long run.

Consider developments in science and technology in recent centuries. In many areas they have made thinkable what was once unthinkable—unthinkable because the experience accumulated in humanity's collective memory left no room for what had never been observed. The sun rose and set. So obvious was that fact that the structures of human language remain unchanged even centuries after it was proven that the earth rotates around the sun. But even though many things once unthinkable are now taken for granted, there remain dark zones in the collective consciousness that have not yet been tackled and won by rational investigation.

It is generally admitted, for example, that all human beings are part of one and the same human species, fellow humans for better or for worse. In relationships between specific human groups, however, that admission does little to change the instinctive mistrust of "the other," whose difference is seen as a threat or an aberration. The identity and coherence of a group takes shape only insofar as it defines its frontiers. Beyond those group frontiers begin the uncertainty and anxiety of difference or chaos.

Increased interchanges between peoples do not yet suffice to constitute humanity as a single grouping. Everywhere the certitudes underlying limited forms of solidarity are so strong that the barriers between sexes, races, religions, lifestyles, and thought patterns remain insurmountable. The "other" is always wrong in being different, even when civility or courtesy compels one to tolerate or accept others as they are. The rules imposed by the necessities of collective life need only be broken for barbarity to break out anew, each group suspecting the other of that tendency. The silence surrounding such barbarous manifestations when they do break out only bears witness to the fragile nature of humanity's progress toward communication with itself as a species.

In the infrastructure of human collective life, in the shadowy zones that might be called the collective unconscious, the certainty of humanity's oneness is a delicate and brittle thing. Our mental structures are not yet geared to creating or promoting humanness on the species level.

Quite aside from the effect of social structures and practices on mental structures, collective certainties themselves remain untouchable or hard to make a dent in. Yet we shall have to tackle them head-on if we really want to organize the collective life of humanity in such a way that a full life becomes possible for all.

A cultural revolution is needed if humanity is to cross the threshold it now faces. The boundaries of all human groups must be enlarged in time and space to take in the whole species. That is a precondition for human survival and a human future, as is stated in the Universal Declaration of Human Rights and in the pacts and conventions designed to implement it legally. Yet most of the real work remains to be done if that viewpoint is to become an accepted reality. All the easy talk about the unity of the human family will become operative only insofar as it shapes the collective unconscious.

Social security, for example, has gradually come to be seen as a necessity for the functioning of industrialized societies. Methods and procedures may be debated, but no one dreams of challenging the principle. What was once regarded as an untimely demand has thus become one of the structures of the collective consciousness.

Today the establishment of a new international economic order is still regarded as a utopia. Yet as far back as 1948, article 28 of the Universal Declaration of Human Rights stipulated: "Everyone is entitled to a social and international order in which the rights and freedoms set forth in this Declaration can be fully realized."

One may lament or revolt against the gap between that statement and the reality. Nevertheless the elaboration of such texts represents an effort by humanity to work upon itself, and in the long run profound change in collective consciousness will depend on such efforts.

Public opinion is an intangible reality open to manipulation. But everyone is beginning to agree that it can become a more powerful force or counterforce than armed might or economic interests when it makes up its mind in the face of situations that have become intolerable to it. Those who hold economic or political power are the most adroit at shaping public opinion, to be sure. But that does not rule out the possibility that public opinion might also be shaped in accordance with the aspirations and demands of those who want a new international order because they are suffering the effects of the prevailing disorder.

To wager on the latter hypothesis is no more illusory than to believe in democracy despite its undeniable decline. Controlled though it may be, information is becoming more general and widespread. This has the effect of enabling all human beings gradually to take cognizance of their right to participate in the management of their collective life. The more that information circulates, the more the public is in a position to raise doubts about the obviousness or legitimacy of the norms and structures imposed upon it.

There can be no society without constraints that are imposed, accepted, or interiorized. But more and more the vast majority of persons in every society will be able to verify the relevance of those necessary constraints. Human beings must do violence to themselves in order to live in society and measure up to truly human standards. And they will more and more be in a position to demand that they be the active subjects or negotiators of that violence. Backward steps are always possible, as history tells us. But that does not make it unreasonable to wager on the growing participation of the majority in the construction of an order to which they are entitled, one that will enable them to live in peace.

Growth in awareness of the exigencies of humanity will come about only if it becomes a goal for all those who are aware of the need to transform the social, political, and economic structures blocking generalized development. Having come to recognize the structural character of underdevelopment, and hence of all development work, they must once again take into account the mental structures and systems of collective assumptions that underlie or cause them. Unquestioned assumptions, certitudes so deeply interiorized that they have become unconscious, do in fact constitute the chief obstacle to transforming the structures that govern relationships between human groupings. So long as the establishment of a new international economic order seems unthinkable or utopian, work on structures through international negotiations will be paralyzed. Governments and international organizations cannot adopt or win ratification for measures that create obligations without the tacit or conscious assent of the peoples they bind by those measures. Contrary to what we might be inclined to think, the fact is that the representatives of public authority, constrained to know what is in the files, are way ahead of public opinion in taking cognizance of the problems that need to be solved and in having the political will to seek out solutions.

What we may also be seeing is the appearance of an international "political class" that is ready to move ahead, but that totally lacks the ability to negotiate solutions with public opinion even though the relevance of such solutions is beyond doubt.

For the whole international dynamic to function, a political will must take shape, particularly in the industrialized countries. It can take shape only when the vast majority realize the need to organize the collective life of humanity. The transition from a focus on nations to a focus on the one human race presupposes the breakdown of nationalist assumptions and certainties. Those assumptions represent the most rigid type of particularism, one imposed by force on ethnic groups constrained to live together. From this standpoint the passionate resistance to any and every form of supranationality is a disturbing indication of humanity's collective impotence at this turning point in its history.

Changing the current representations of development and underdevelopment will be no less necessary than enlarging the frontiers within which human groups envision and organize their collective life. Although it is fashionable to smile at it, the myth of progress continues to exercise a determining influence on our picture of human history. We continue to see it as a caravan, with those up front infallibly tracing out the route. Underdevelopment is seen as nothing more than the stage prior to development. It is a state of distress from which nations can escape only by taking the road to development, by following the road opened by others who have succeeded with *their* "development."

The inertia and snares of language are particularly indicative of the work that remains to be done if the reorganization of the world is to become thinkable. And such reorganization is needed if development for all peoples is to be feasible.

Chapter 2

Underdevelopment and Development: Analysis of Causes and Problems

Although negotiations to establish a new international economic order have reached an impasse, the years when they occupied center stage in world politics were not entirely wasted. Those years saw a collective advance in our analysis of underdevelopment and the conditions required for generalized development.

We began to realize that underdevelopment cannot be regarded simply as the situation prior to development. Instead underdevelopment is always a process of disintegration resulting from some antecedent process of development. In peripheral societies, for example, underdevelopment is due to the development of the societies at the center of the system—the system itself resulting from the organization and expansion of the central societies.

Thus the precondition for development is not the mere transfer of development resources from the center to the periphery. It includes the activation of the periphery through the conscientization of underdeveloped peoples, the restructuring of societies, the voluntary transformation of the global system, and the conscientization of peoples in highly developed nations. The political will of the latter would suffice to render development both feasible and necessary.

Thesis 4: Underdevelopment is not explained by technological backwardness.

One of the assumptions most difficult to uproot is the identification of underdevelopment with technological backwardness. Indeed that apparent connection had much to do with the coinage of the word "underdevelopment" and with the images and concept underlying it. Persons from industrialized countries noticed the absence of even the most elementary technical facilities in "underdeveloped" countries, facilities that they could not imagine themselves doing without—for example, roads; the use of fossil, hydraulic, mechanical, and electrical energy; means of transportation; long-distance communication.

We are so aware of the utility of such technical facilities that we tend to forget how recently most of them were invented. We find it hard to imagine that other human groups could and did live humanely without having access to such facilities. It is even more difficult for us to realize that the absence of such failities among certain human groups can be explained by the fact that there was no felt need for them. Other techniques and resources were implemented to resolve problems faced by the social group. Paleontology, archeology, and ethnography have informed us how often and how well the most diverse human groups have succeeded in living in extremely hostile environments. On polar ice, on deserts, and in virgin forests they made the best of the elements at their disposal and found ingenious answers to their concrete problems. In many instances so-called primitive cultures remain unsurpassable, even though modern societies may seem to have arrived at more satisfactory solutions by various circuitous routes.

The civilization that began to take shape in Europe around the twelfth century C.E. was the heir of earlier civilizations and their contributions: Greco-Roman civilization, Muslim civilization, Chinese civilization. But European civilization has imposed its model on the world to such an extent that it has erased much from the collective memory of humankind. We have forgotten all the bold feats that enabled human beings to achieve humanity during the long millennia that preceded the last few centuries of "progress." The domestication of the horse and the dog, the resolution of problems caused by tropical humidity, the use of irrigation for rice cultivation, the mastery of poisonous substances, the organization of social life through kinship structures and languages—all these represent achievements of the utmost importance. Only at our peril may we forget that it was through such achievements that humankind won its humanness.

Research workers are now taking cognizance of this fact and are trying to preserve memorabilia that may be endangered by interference and manipulation motivated by other interests. But it is not just a matter of stocking our museums with vestiges of the past; it is also a matter of looking out for the future. In animal selection and breeding, for example, breeders now try to preserve the original stocks that are being crossed, lest the resultant hybrids degenerate and they have to start over again. On the other side of the coin, changes in the use of land in certain woodland areas has had such an impact on climate and other factors that specialists have been compelled to give more serious thought to the way space was organized by peoples of an earlier day.

The rediscovery of forgotten human achievements is not just useful for a better knowledge of history and prehistory, and for a more prudent approach to the future. It is needed if we are to comprehend the reality known as "underdevelopment" and to take correct steps toward development.

The problem of sound development would be relatively simple to solve if the achievements of the so-called developed societies were, in every respect, not only the best but also the only imaginable ones once they became a reality. We would only have to transfer, inculcate, or impose them on underdeveloped nations, teaching them the knowledge, technology, and know-how elaborated in the developed countries. Indeed that is generally how work for development has been conceived and envisioned. Those who know are to go out and educate those who do not know. In many instances results have been far from convincing, but that did not call the approach itself into question. Failures were blamed on students and apprentices, who were clearly unfit to make progress.

Here we have a typical example of a mental structure shaped by one particular history posing a seemingly insurmountable obstacle to the comprehension of human reality as a whole. The matter seems simple enough if one interprets it as a process of evolution whose direction is clearly indicated by the achievements of the developed countries. It becomes much richer and more complicated if one tries to follow the many different courses that humanity has taken in seeking fulfilment. It is far from obvious that all those human pathways are doomed to be absorbed in the course called "modernity." And even if that were the case, it is to be hoped that other human approaches would find enrichment and fulfilment in the process rather than have their own achievements lost in oblivion. For those achievements might prove to be valuable some day.

So we must try to comprehend the earlier history of various peoples, their history before they fell prey to underdevelopment. It is not that we have a relish for folklore. Such understanding is needed if we are to define the conditions of development. If underdevelopment is not simply the stage prior to development, then we are forced to conclude that *there was a stage prior to underdevelopment in the history of every nation or people*. No society would keep reproducing itself for millennia in a state of underdevelopment. Human societies reproduce themselves from one generation to the next only insofar as they manage to produce the conditions for their existence, and all human societies come from a long succession of ages. Until the last few millennia at least, communication between them was such that they all had to do their own work. Each had to fashion the images, techniques, and organizations needed to keep existing, functioning, and transmitting experience to the upcoming generation.

To be sure, we cannot fully grasp the prehistory and history of humanity as a whole: our knowledge always remains incomplete and biased. But once we make an effort in that direction, it becomes clear that our current images may be quite wrong, that the backwardness of one society vis-à-vis another is a relative matter, to say the very least. No society serves as the undisputed standard for all the others.

When European expansion began in the fifteenth century, the relativity of civilizations was more perceptible than it is today, of course. The nations that were to become the agents of "progress" were less sure of their superiority over other peoples than their successors would be. Indeed one of the motives for their dynamic outreach was their desire to discover and possess the marvels of other realms. If we are to understand underdevelopment, we must rediscover that sense of curiosity, that feeling of wonderment for the achievements of others— whether they be merely different, complementary, or superior.

The history of every human society is the combined product of memory and imagination. It is the accumulation and prolongation of experience along a more or less continous line. Breaks in that trajectory can serve as occasions for progress. Every society constructs and reproduces itself by organizing to interrelate its experiences and the discoveries that enrich its tradition without overturning it. A certain balance or coherence must be maintained if life is to continue. Thus the reproduction of social and mental structures from one generation to the next is not necessarily a sign of sclerosis. It may epitomize a perfect balancing of accumulated experience. It is said that happy peoples have no history. It seems to me that the perpetuation of gestures, procedures, representations, and the like may be the sign of their relevance. If the crucial problems of life are solved thereby, by what criterion can one talk about "backwardness"?

That sort of comparative evaluation is beside the point here, however, for that is not where our real problem lies. What we must come to realize is the fact that many peoples of the world who have entered a stage of underdevelopment, who are threatened with death and annihilation, spent centuries and millennia finding satisfactory solutions for their basic needs. They managed to find food and protection, to organize their society, and to gain some understanding of the world and human destiny. Peoples that have benefited from technical progress tend to project a picture of want and poverty onto their own past and that of other peoples. Thanks to technology, they feel, that terrible past was overcome. The picture is not entirely illusory, but neither may the poverty have been exactly what they imagine. Scarcity of goods and the feeling of abandonment in the world of nature may well have characterized human beginnings. But from the very start human beings tackled and surmounted those realities, shaping their lives from one century to the next.

I am not suggesting that we return to the myth of the "noble savage" living in an earthly paradise during some golden age, which does remain a structure in the collective unconscious. The point is that humanity, ever since its appearance on earth, has persistently managed to work out its existence in an environment that did not ensure its continuing survival. Humankind has been in a *process of development* ever since its appearance, struggling to master nature and the basic prerequisites for survival. All its achievements have helped to consolidate its chances for survival. Many of those achievements may lie buried and forgotten now, but that is only because they are less operational at this point.

Before underdevelopment came along, therefore, there was development. And it was different from the sort of development that has come to seem obligatory since technological societies became so much more powerful than others that they have extended their patterns of human effort and achievement and wiped out other patterns.

"Backwardness," then, really has to do with ratios of power. Those societies with the most power impose their patterns on other societies: not only their way of thinking and doing things but also their way of interpreting history and the course of human evolution. Their advanced status is their self-image, which they then force upon others. It is a reflection of their power and domination. They are right: they are the standard and model, because they are the stronger. The victor's norm wipes out all recollection of the lengthy efforts that every people had to make in order to develop its humanity.

Traditional societies were able to lean upon their past for support because they appreciated the value of the lessons it had taught them. Insofar as they now focus too much on the future, they are in danger of losing their identity and sinking irreversibly into underdevelopment.

Thesis 5: The underdevelopment of some is the result of the development of others.

Granting that the underdeveloped countries were in a process of development before they succumbed to underdevelopment, we must now ask what accident disturbed their process of evolution. What interrupted the processes that enabled those societies to reproduce themselves generation after generation, renewing themselves by necessary adaptations to changes in their environment as they went along? The accident could be either internal or external in origin. It could be due to biological or cultural degeneration; or it could be due to outside intervention.

In general, the disorganization of societies seems to me to be the effect of outside influence or intervention, of contact with a society undergoing expansion and hence in a position of force. In each individual case, to be sure, one must evaluate the extent to which the outside intervention was debilitative or stimulative. In contacts between different societies the influence of the dominant society may be a spur to innovation and cultural enrichment; or it may cause upset and anemia. Phenomena akin to present-day underdevelopment have certainly occurred throughout human history. The only traces left to us are generally those in the culture of the dominators: the winners write the history books.

On the whole, current underdevelopment around the world is the result of the development and expansion of European societies since the fifteenth century. It is that specific underdevelopment we must try to understand and appreciate fully, because humanity must now come to grips with it in order to fashion its future.

The problem is that we find it difficult to get beyond the collective certitudes that prevail in both developed and underdeveloped countries. Public opinion can hardly gainsay the civilizing work of industrialized countries around the world as they sought to reorganize that world. The whole world, whether it likes it or not, is following in their footsteps. Their model has the force of law, even when it is challenged in the most radical way. Its breakup as the result of internal contradictions, in both its socialist and liberal capitalist forms, only further accentuates its obviousness and certainty, and renders critical analysis impossible. But sometime or other we must get down to critically analyzing the irrationality that characterizes the model in its relationships with nature and the totality of human history. We must consider its irresponsible exploitation of relatively limited resources and its de facto rejection of much of human experience accumulated over millennia.

Achievements in the mastery of nature, the organization of collective life, and the enhancement of cultural life are taken so much for granted that the concomitant ravages tend to be regarded as the price that must be paid for any and all beneficial transformations of reality. The assured satisfaction of basic needs, progress in medicine, education, and information-gathering, and the possibility of large numbers of persons enjoying an affluence once reserved to an elite are viewed as signs of enormous progress. When one alludes to the price that *others* had to pay to make that progress possible, the reaction is prompt and negative. It is as if one were profaning the god of an ardent believer. And the problem is compounded by the fact that the unselfishness and generosity of some promoters of our civilization have, with good reason, been held up as praiseworthy and exemplary.

But we must examine the hidden face of the civilizing or colonial venture, even at the risk of stirring up guilt feelings that may cause some to resist even more vehemently a careful analysis of reality. That dark side is inextricably bound up with the construction of industrial society. Its impact on other societies has been destructive as well as constructive. It may have induced other societies to follow in its footsteps, but it also seriously disturbed the dynamics of their productive and reproductive processes.

Expanding industrial society intervened in the rest of the world to expropriate the resources needed for its processes of transformation and consumption, even when it went above and beyond the satisfaction of basic needs. Although the term continues to be disputed, there is talk of the "looting" of the Third World. And there is no denying that the industrialized nations have gone there to find the resources they need. It is equally true that most of those resources were unclaimed. Because the indigenous population did not know how to transform them and make them useful, they had no use and hence no value. It is true that some of those resources had already been exploited for local consumption or prestige. Some agricultural products provided basic foods and condiments: rice, manioc, spices. Others provided clothing: cotton, wool. Still other resources, such as precious minerals, were hoarded as treasures or used to flaunt social status and prestige. We must also remember that the exploitation of some resources (e.g., minerals and coffee) inevitably turned part of the population away from the production of basic foodstuffs without providing them with the means to procure those foodstuffs cheaply. But the basic fact remains: most of the resources in the Third World were of no use until industry would transform them into commodities.

That fact rules out the possibility of explaining underdevelopment solely in terms of the plunder of resources, even if we grant the fact that the exhaustion and disappearance of resources does constitute a handicap for the country in question. To take an example outside the Third World, consider the case of Brittany. Phoenician and Roman exploitation of its tin and silver-bearing lead does not explain its relative underdevelopment. Other factors must be taken into account: Colbert's policies of centralism and protectionism, the industrialization of textile production in Great Britain, and so forth. All those factors helped to disrupt the relationship between agriculture and textile handicraft, so that Brittany came to depend on the production and processing of hemp and flax. Today it is admired for its "provincial charm."

But even though the exploitation of resources does not suffice to explain underdevelopment, we certainly must take into account the conditions under which that exploitation was carried out.

By force or domination the industrializing countries stepped in to interfere with the life of other countries. The latter would come to constitute the "periphery" of a world "united" around a "center" where capital, production activities, and power were concentrated. Granted that serious analysis must strip the correlative concepts of domination and dependence of all sentimental connotations, the fact remains that we must carefully consider the place to be given to those concepts in any explanation of underdevelopment.

The first point to be noted is that a relationship of domination or dependence is always a reciprocal one. One human group truly dominates another only insofar as the latter consents to it. So long as it resists foreign domination, it is not really dependent. From that standpoint we must make a distinction between the colonization of a country and its occupation by a foreign power. Although the transition from occupation to colonization can be subtly effected with the complicity or collaboration of indigenous factions, it is also true historically that resistance to occupation has often served to transform foreign intervention by sparking anew the inner dynamism of the occupied country. But generally speaking, and despite domestic resistance and its repression, we can say that the domination of the world by expanding industrial societies has been carried out in such a way that the dominated nations found themselves in a situation of dependence, if for no other reason than the fact that any potential resistance was doomed to failure from the very start.

To the extent that dependent nations acquiesced willy-nilly in their dependence, they found themselves stripped of mastery over their own dynamics, turned into satellites, and polarized around the expansion and organization of the dominant society. All decisions affecting their collective life would stem from the dominant society. Having no control over the conditions surrounding their own internal organization, they could only adapt to the demands imposed by the economic, social, and political structures of the dominant society. Living on the margins of the global society taking shape, they could offer no resistance to the effects of the worldwide system that was giving them form and structure.

It is to this mechanism or relationship of domination/dependence that we must look if we wish to find the starting point for a sound explanation of underdevelopment. We must examine carefully and precisely how underdevelopment results from the reality of that relationship. But even before we analyze the effects of dependence, we must consider how dependence is created in the first place.

Societies are fashioned out of a network of basic, constitutive relationships—for example, those created by the exchange of goods, material or symbolic, and of services, resulting from a division of labor or from a wide variety of activities, needs, and tastes. Insofar as the forming of those relationships takes shape day after day in and through the life of various groups, a society can manage to find its own regulatory criteria. There may be internal conflicts and contradictions. There may be internal relationships of domination/dependence. But on the whole the society in question maintains some control over the factors governing the negotiation or transformation of those matters.

The situation is very different when there is an external relationship of domination/dependence. When a society finds itself more and more determined from the outside, its constituent groups are polarized by the dominant society. The arrangement of iron filings on a sheet of paper when a magnet is placed under it is a good image of that polarization. We can see the same image repeated on a map or a satellite photograph: in a given country all activity may be polarized around one port city that has become the bridgehead of the dominant society.

Stripped of their resources and determined by extraneous factors, the underdeveloped societies of the periphery find their center displaced. It can reach the point where their own center, the pole around which they are structured, is none other than the industrial center that is organizing the world in terms of its own needs, interests, and contradictions.

In that case the development of the center, far from being the source of development for the periphery, becomes the chief factor in its underdevelopment. In organizing itself, it disorganizes the rest of the world. It is not unthinkable, of course, that in the long run such a process of universal gravitation might lead to overall development everywhere. But we can no longer pursue that dream without taking into account the short-term or middle-term disaggregation involved. For the disintegrative effects are the only ones perceptible to those societies that are suffering and dying from them.

When citizens of the industrialized nations talk about "helping the Third World," they often mean that they are ready to show it the right road to follow. Hence it is absolutely necessary that they be confronted with an analysis of the hidden face of their own development, with the price that their ancestors had to pay in order to make it possible. Action in behalf of development is in danger of prolonging the polarization of dependent countries if it is not accompanied by an elucidation of the mechanisms that are perpetuating their dependence.

Thesis 6: Underdevelopment is the destructuring of a society, resulting from its polarization by another, dominant society.

When dependent societies are polarized by a dominant society, their structure crumbles. They are "destructured." Their organizations, shaped over centuries to handle relationships between groups, begin to collapse insofar as they are polarized or determined by outside forces. Underdevelopment is nothing other than this destructuring process.

We need not say anything here about the exact course of that process. Whatever it may be, it eventually affects every aspect and dimension of social organization. The result is the same, whether it begins with shifts in the image of the deity or with changes in production relationships. For an initial approach to the phenomenon, then, it matters little in what order the various aspects are presented.

The introduction of cultural or medical techniques, which have passed the test in the industrialized countries, renders obsolete the inherited techiques of autochthonous tradition. Knowledge and mastery of those techniques are lost. Only too late is it realized that the old techniques were adequate to meet the needs of the situation. One thinks, for example, of the rudimentary reaper perfected by Gallic tribes unfamiliar with slavery, various forms of terraced farming, and the agricultural exploitation of saltlands. It is in the field of medicine, in particular, that the loss of traditional techniques is liable to be discovered too late. One need only think of the use of acupuncture (preserved in China), the treatment of certain mental illnesses, and the many techniques of which all memory has been lost.

More serious than the obsolescence of techniques, however, is the obsolescence of human beings. In their own eyes they see themselves as having lost their qualifications and competence. I recall an African agronomist's reply to certain clerics who had been expostulating on the ignorance of the rural poor. He said, "The peasant is the first and foremost agronomist." It brings out clearly the whole problem raised for a human group when there is a break in the transmission of techniques, when discontinuity enters the picture.

More directly visible is the often brutal transformation of the modes of production and of the organization of economic activity, and their effects on society. From producing commodities for the satisfaction of basic needs, dependent societies must shift to providing manual labor for business enterprises designed to meet the demands of industrialized nations and bring large profits to their owners. Working on plantations, in mines, or in refineries, indigenous farmers and artisans become proletarian in two ways: they produce goods whose use is wholly alien to them, and they receive salaries that rule out their access to those goods. It is the same story whether we are talking about wine produced by Muslims or uranium extracted by nomads. And at times they end up with imported farm tools completely unsuited to their own agricultural needs. Integration into the worldwide market economy establishes an insurmountable distance between workers and the goods they help to produce. Meanwhile the world is no longer in a position to provide the basic goods that would ensure their subsistence.

The food dependence of the Third World, which grows more serious each year, is a consequence of this disjointed economy. The use of manioc to feed European livestock and the raising of sugar cane to produce alcohol for use in car motors are only two examples of this perversion in economic processes.

It goes without saying that this extraversion of economic activity disorganizes social relationships. The societal dualism it fosters between a traditional sector and a modern sector is merely the visible face of the disintegration of domestic social structures. The equilibrium of a region, a village, or an extended family comes apart as those seeking employment are drawn to the cities. There they are often forced to live in shantytowns, or as parasites on their elder brothers and sisters who have had the chance to become integrated into the new system. This parasitism, which so stuns observers, is a residue of the broad-based solidarity that was present in traditional society. Before underdevelopment came, the structure of indigenous society gave everyone a place, ensuring their socialization and demanding their responsible participation in collective tasks. Traditional society was highly structured. The adequate functioning of systems of relationships built up over the centuries is what ensured their transmission and reproduction from generation to generation. The disorganization of social relationships epitomizes most fully the destructuring of societies—underdevelopment. Society is no longer in a position to maintain itself.

Politics may be regarded as the ordering of a society through the imposition of certain necessary constraints on all, constraints that are acceptable to all. Obviously a basic distortion is introduced into this process when a society is shaped from outside itself. Norms and structures are imposed that mean nothing to the members of the society in question. Forced submission or resignation takes the place of the approval or consensus that is necessary for civic life.

To be sure, this political alienation is not peculiar to colonized or underdeveloped countries. It is also to be found in any society where there is no real, effective democracy. But the outside, foreign nature of power and authority accentuates the process of destructuring at work in underdeveloped countries and brings out more clearly their loss of control. Caught up in the dynamics of expanding industrial society, dependent societies lose all control over their own inner dynamics. The disintegration of some societies after winning their independence is merely the long-term effect of this destructuring process; it is not a sign of their immaturity or their unreadiness for self-determination.

The disorganization of cultures and thought patterns, whether it be the effect or one of the causes of this social destructuring, disturbs groups and individuals down to their unconscious depths where collective patterns of behavior are shaped. The ideological authority of the dominant society, rooted in the force underpinning its domination, annuls the wisdom and experience transmitted by tradition, often making it look ridiculous even in the eyes of the local population. The native heritage no longer seems to have sense or value, whereas the dominant model is impressive by virtue of its proven efficacy. Seemingly doomed to identify itself with the stronger, more masterful society, a dependent people loses its identity. It no longer knows who it is. Its reference points and sources no longer speak to it, even though it may remain focused on those sources without daring to admit it.

Viewed in this perspective, the worldwide movement to get back to ancestral roots should not be scorned or underestimated. If it is not an ambiguous quest for refuge from the hard facts of life, it may well represent the centuries-long resistance of human groups to the alienation caused by uprooting. And if it does not come too late, it may serve as the starting point for a process of restructuring destructured societies. A group's self-awareness is one of the sources of its organization as a group.

Religious structures, as organizing influences on representations or behavior patterns, may well be the last structures to be dislodged—even though they may seem to be the first affected by foreign intervention in the form of christianization or islamization. The transformation of individual or group relationships to a deity or deities, or of their representations of the divine, takes away the last obstacle on the road to development or underdevelopment.

Without doubt the sacralization of social organizations, a process still poorly understood, is the one that makes the most radical contribution to societal structuring. The constraints required for the functioning of societal life are seen as imperative only when they become self-evident, when they are viewed as somehow bound up with a relationship to the divine.

In that sense the "divinization of Caesar" is not an aberration but an almost necessary or fated part of social dynamics. Power has something of the divine or diabolic about it. Though it is always fashioned by human hands, it imposes itself on human beings only to the extent that it escapes their control. Nothing may be more dangerous to the advancement of human beings in freedom, but nothing may be more inevitable in the construction of societies.

When change becomes necessary, it cannot be accomplished without desacralizing certain solid structures. But even if that be true, the point is that the way in which the process of desacralization is carried out is not a matter of indifference. The negation or profanation of a people's relationship to the divine, be it by Christianity, Marxism, or positivism, is not necessarily the best way to gain the needed control over the sacred upon which the transformation of religious conduct will depend. Such transformation may lead to a crisis that can prove to be fatal. In all likelihood it is at this deep level, scarcely noticeable even to those involved, that much of the drama of societal disintegration is lived out.

At every level of social activity, then, underdevelopment is a destructuring process. It is the disintegration of relationships that were built up over centuries and enabled a given society to exist. The overall network of interrelated subunits that constitutes a functioning society becomes a mere conglomerate of unrelated individuals and groups. Polarized by the dominant society, they may be able to restructure themselves around it in the long run; but in so doing, they will become increasingly dependent and marginal.

Societal life is always undergoing transformation, of course. Relationships between groups and individuals are always changing with modifications in the environment, technology, modes of production, mental representations, and so forth. What sets off underdevelopment is the fact that the destructuring of a society is caused by an outside force, and that the society in question has no possibility of controlling the process.

I have treated the disintegration of societal relationships in an almost mathematically abstract way. In real life that disintegration can degenerate to the point where the members of a society become little more than vagrants and hobos. When societies are stripped of mastery over their constitutive relationships, individuals are left to themselves and may end up letting themselves die. Ethnocide, one form of underdevelopment, may sometimes end in genocide: physical death follows from the disintegration of a universe that had been built up over generations to provide the necessities of life.

Thesis 7: Conscientization is the first precondition for the development of a repressed people.

If underdevelopment is the destructuring of a society, then development necessarily entails a process of restructuring. Although the process may be triggered from outside, it really begins only when the basic, constitutive groups in a society take in hand the reorganization of the relationships that structure their collective life. They must take some initiative in their own change, and they must take active cognizance of it. If underdevelopment leads to resignation, fatalism, despair, or revolt, development begins with the realization that it is possible to do something, to become once again an active agent in the social process.

Dependence, impotence, and poverty do not flow necessarily from the nature of things, from some divine order. But that fact is not self-evident to persons who have always lived under such conditions, who have been told repeatedly that such is their lot here below, and who have met with nothing but failure in their efforts to get beyond that situation. If they have managed to survive, it is because they have used the resources available to them to overcome the obstacles placed in their way by the systems of relationships imposed on them.

Around the Mediterranean, in the Andes, and in the Philippines, societies have built terraces to produce their basic necessities. In most cases, however, they were forced to do so by the pressure of invasions and forced tributes. They have managed to survive in such places against all odds because they created the basic conditions needed to produce their means of subsistence. But there is a limit to such creative leaps by a community. There comes a point when weariness takes hold. The group prefers to give way to illusions that make survival tolerable rather than continue to achieve the seemingly impossible.

Insofar as the group continues to reproduce itself, however, new generations appear on the scene. Unfamiliar with previous failures, they are ready to try something new at home or head out for someplace else. If newly imagined initiatives are not quashed by the inertia of the older generation, or if they are given outside backing, then the group can get a grip on reality once again and mobilize to take control over it.

Outside intervention, if it is not restricted to the mere popularization of new tools, new techniques, or new modes of production, may also serve to stimulate or promote conscientization. If there is some minimum analysis of historical or structural factors affecting a group's living conditions, the group may find new chances to comprehend its situation and to mobilize itself for the task of regaining control over its problems. Many conditions must be met, however, before such a process can be successful. The outsiders cannot simply step in to teach what they know. They must be familiar with the group from the inside, join with it in exploring its community memory, and win acceptance as fellow companions in the process. Precisely because they are from the outside, only then can they stimulate the community to its own research and innovation. It is as fellow seekers that they can help the local community to envision certain initiatives as feasible, initiatives that may have seemed unthinkable before. Such a process of dialogue may gradually enable the group to take its own affairs in hand once more.

Training in new techniques can serve as the occasion for conscientization of that sort, but conscientization itself is a much more comprehensive process. It entails some analysis of the relationships that structure a group, both within and without. Literacy training, for example, is not necessarily a conscientization process. But it can become so if it is conducted along the lines of Paulo Freire's approach, if it encourages an analysis of reality by getting the students to discover the linguistic structures that shape the reading process and mirror societal realities.

Let me cite two other examples. Learning to read scales need not be conscientization, but it can be if it enables customers to know when they are being cheated on weights and prices. If a veterinarian does not explain what he is doing to treat an animal, if he conceals his techniques in order to perpetuate the need that others have for him, then he is obviously working against the process of conscientization. He may help it along, on the other hand, if he encourages others to study and learn the know-how of his practice.

Once some group becomes aware of its ability to transform its situation, it enters a new set of dynamics. In the French-speaking world, we call it "self-reliance," because we have no French word to express the matter precisely. Americans talk about "pulling yourself up by your own bootstraps." In contrast to a situation of dependence on outsiders, a self-reliant group depends on itself to promote and regulate the activities of its communal life. It makes its own decisions, engages in self-determination. This may not mean autarchy or complete self-sufficiency, but it does mean that the group controls its relationships with the outside world sufficiently to avoid falling back into dependence. It does as much as it can to maintain control over acculturation, extraversion, and polarization by the center of the system. It reconstructs itself as a social group or society. Its internal relationships are cohesive enough to prevent it from being totally defined by its relationships to the dominant group of which it had been a satellite.

Such a process of social restructuring is necessarily a long-term one. The effects of destructuring are not abolished by the decision to regain autonomy, even if a group goes so far as to break off relationships and choose "voluntary quarantine." The allure and effectiveness of the dominant model will continue to have an impact, even after the decision for self-determination has been made.

Decision-making implies the voluntarism involved in self-reliance and the conscientization that leads to it. Herein lies the whole problem of development, even though all the preconditions for it may still not be at hand. Once a group takes cognizance of the possibility and necessity of self-determination, and once it decides to become an active agent in its own development again, then it has found a point of departure for mastering the conditions surrounding its existence.

Modernization is indeed possible without such a starting point, and it may even lead to economic growth. But in such a case it is likely that the process of destructuring and underdevelopment will only accelerate. Development can be only a chancy byproduct of the group's marginal integration into the dominant society.

Every real process of development begins with a process of reactivation or cultural revolution. Groups enmeshed in underdevelopment must become producers of their own culture and their own history once again. The return to native roots and the reconstruction of communal identity and memory can pave the way for such a renaissance.

But such a renaissance depends, in the last analysis, on a communal will to self-determination and self-creation. Improbable and transitory as such phenomena seem to be, they do occur; and they tend to be on the increase right now.

Having explored the ins and outs of the "obvious" and common view that humanity is more a product of history than its maker, many are being led beyond that view to further questions. All things considered, must we not say that humanity is, after all, the agent of its own history? Is it not so at least potentially or by vocation? Is this not evident in the role played by those who open its eyes to new alternatives?

Careful analysis of underdevelopment and the practice of development enable us to glimpse new perspectives. They are less disenchanted—but certainly not illusory—than those that suggest that all individual and collective conduct is determined by a system whose ascendancy grows even as its centers of power become increasingly intangible. What we are seeing in dependent societies, which now have little or no say in the decisions affecting the course of their history, is a growing movement to acquire some minimal mastery over the situation so that they can undertake a restructuring process.

Inasmuch as dependent societies were the first to be affected by destructuration, they may also be the first to be forced to regain their relative autonomy and self-determination. And as the effects of the destructuring process flow back toward the center of the system, the underdeveloped nations may find themselves destined to open new pathways for humanity in producing and controlling the prerequisites for its collective life.

Developing societies, then, must analyze and reinterpret their history, their traditions, the shattered elements of their inherited structures, their culture and religion, and their relationships to surrounding or dominant societies. It is an enormous, long-term task. But on the basis of observable data I should say it is not impossible for groups that are determined to survive and revive. Conscientization has reached such a pitch in the underdeveloped nations that the poor and the neglected are once again on the verge of making history, just as the powerful are confronting an impasse and the complete breakdown of the global system.

Aid to the Third World, taken so much for granted by those who think they hold the key to success, will have to give way to something else: the conscientization of peoples in industrialized nations by already conscientized groups in the underdeveloped nations. This reversal of relationships is not as unthinkable as it may seem, and in fact it is already in progress. The victims of a badly twisted world are in a good position to point up its mistakes and effects. A system that produces and maintains underdevelopment can be dismantled only by those whose very life depends on fashioning different systems of social interaction.

Thesis 8: Development is a process of societal restructuration; it presupposes the recovery of self-government.

The decolonization of the 1960s was often experienced by dependent peoples as a reconquest of their dignity and identity. Supposedly destined for full assimilation or integration into the global system, they reappropriated their own memory. They could now assimilate ideas and techniques from the outside world and engage in innovation by reinterpreting them in terms of their own innate dynamics. Thus decolonization was a cultural process, even though effects of the dominant culture are still in evidence.

More radically, the negotiation or conquest of independence was political, and was intended to be so, even though self-determination was often illusory or merely formal insofar as the older dependent relationships of the colonial era were reproduced or even reinforced. Newly established authorities were often linked with new or old centers and continued to function along the lines of the old administrative model.

The fact remains that the social reconstruction of a nation depends upon a people's governing itself. The construction and implementation of a power apparatus marks a first step in restoring an interior, domestic axis for restructuring all the subunits in a country polarized by another, dominant society. As it pursues real independence, this power apparatus must also help to restore interrelationships between the subunits. All too often, unfortunately, groups in power have a vested interest in maintaining the old circuits of dependence and so they do nothing but conceal their perpetuation. Independence is then illusory, and societal destructuring continues.

When the power apparatus is controlled by individuals and groups determined to implement a policy of development, however, then the power apparatus can become the starting point for new relationships in and between groups—relationships that will help to satisfy their basic needs and foster their identity. The dynamics of self-reliance or self-determination can be unleashed, acquiring the needed means as it goes along. Acting in tension with the movement of conscientization among elementary groups, the power apparatus can serve as the agent of the violence that every society must do to itself in order to be built. But one condition must be met for this to be the case. Either by election or by tacit consent, the power apparatus must emanate from the constituency it is trying to hold together.

The state apparatus must analyze and know about the complementary and seemingly contradictory interactions between the various groups that are constrained to live together. It can then be organized in such a way as to think out, articulate, and implement a suitable strategy or policy for coordinating the initiatives of groups that are once again taking charge of their own affairs. Insofar as it does what it can to maintain control over foreign relations and the outside world that had been manipulating domestic community life, it can help to structure the nation's overall life in new terms. Those terms would be based on the new relationships being forged between domestic groups that are breaking with the dependence model and hence capable of complementing one another.

Such a policy can only be voluntary. It must entail programing and planning a national life for the groups involved. Up to now they have coexisted only within the framework of dependence on the dominant society outside. But that submission to an outside power helped to create ties of cooperation between different local groups, and those ties may serve as the starting point for new, complementary relationships. Although maintaining the old colonial boundaries, for example, heads of African nations are aware of their arbitrariness and their historical import. Those boundaries often broke through older ethnic and interethnic relationships. The only problem is that changing boundaries again might sunder other relationships if governments seek the bases of their national construction too far in space or time past.

A policy of development is possible only if it brings together, in sufficient space, human groups large enough and diversified enough to ensure that their complementary interaction will produce the basic equilibrium needed to ensure the exchanges of goods and services that structure a society. Insofar as national or regional ties of interdependence do not alter the circuits of foreign dependence, polarization by the dominant society will continue to produce its destructuring effects. The collective, regional, or international autonomy of the developing countries will undoubtedly become the basic strategy for breaking the dependency cycle, even if it should be confined to the satisfaction of basic needs. Having been tributaries of the industrialized countries insofar as manufactured products are concerned, the developing countries cannot now let themselves go on being dependent on those same countries for the satisfaction of their food needs. If they do, they will only become more securely locked into dependence.

Access to independence is not, however, limited to breaking the cycle of dependence. A precondition for real independence is the construction of systems of interrelationships that will render some degree of self-sufficiency possible. Such independence will be relative, of course, but some degree of independence is necessary so that a society may function to satisfy the needs of its population as best it can.

This is the chief task of government: to fashion society in those terms. It was often the role claimed by warlords, princes, or religious leaders who had enough physical or ideological force to impose their views or their norms on the people they governed. Today the situation is different, however slow the shift to democracy may be. More and more it is the relevance or credibility of views, laws, and plans that will have to be used to endow governments with the authority they need to impose themselves on their nations. The violence needed to coordinate human groups in a society will have to be imposed by negotiation. Decisions will have to be explained, information will have to be provided about new perspectives and future prospects, and the collective consciousness will have to be trained and educated. Otherwise governments will have to resort to institutional violence, and sooner or later their citizens will revolt.

There is another reason why the necessary measure of violence for restructuring societies cannot be imposed externally. Independence movements have engraved the will to self-determination on the collective consciousness. As processes of conscientization and self-reliance take on shape and consistency, linkage between the restructuring of societies and their control by a governmental power apparatus will become increasingly necessary—and increasingly difficult to negotiate. Thus the reorganization of destructured societies bears witness once again to one of the paradoxes of political life: strong authorities and powers are needed to force societal construction; but they will endure only if citizens give their adhesion, consenting to the delegation of the authority needed to assert themselves.

These contradictions are scarcely resolved in the succession of coups d'etat that plague the Third World. Far from cushioning such contradictions, the coups merely accentuate them. But contrary to what many in the old metropolitan countries think, those chain-reaction coups are not further proof that colonized nations have no aptitude for self-determination. Instead they spotlight the theoretical and practical difficulty of establishing compatibility between strong authority on the one hand and the voluntary mobilization of a nation's citizens on the other.

Thus the function of inspiring and conscientizing the populace becomes just as important for governments as their organizational and administrative functions. They must make every effort to render credible the constraints that must be imposed, taking care to have those constraints dovetail with real needs as much as possible. Consider, for example, the effort to stabilize the price of a product that has been doing well on the world market over a period of years. If the transfer of its gains to other sectors of the economy is to be possible, there cannot be excessive resistance from producers who are being deprived of short-term profits for the sake of greater security in lean years. To forestall such resistance, the government must be able to explain and justify its overall policy, to prove its value and relevance over a longer period of time. It is easy to see how strictly and carefully such a policy must be carried out if it is to be credible to those who are paying the price for it right now. In the industrialized countries, be they capitalist or socialist, transfers of capital from agriculture to the industrial and service sectors have generally been made without any real regard for the sensibilities of those involved.

Such functions endow governments with an ideological power and authority that could become exorbitant if it is not balanced by the conscientization and self-organization of the people. It is in the tension between these two countervailing powers that the restructuring of disintegrated societies can be carried out.

Thesis 9: The prerequisite for generalized development is the transformation of the global system, of which underdevelopment is the inevitable result.

Public opinion has been sensitized to the hazards of industrialization and urbanization by a variety of obvious facts: befouled shorelines and other examples of pollution; wind and water erosion resulting from short-sighted use of land; the potential exhaustion of certain resources in the near future; and so forth. Humanity is in danger of losing control over such processes for having failed to worry early enough about how to cope with them.

We must, of course, ponder forecasts of catastrophes that would paralyze societies insofar as we might not be able to reintegrate them into a harmonious "natural" life. But it is no less necessary for us to realize that there is a future to be thought out and planned, to be managed responsibly as a whole in which all elements are interdependent.

The proliferation of efforts to get the maximum results from available resources does not necessarily involve their proper coordination. Not only do various business activities run counter to one another, but their joining together can become a threat to all the others. Chain reactions in nature are such that interference with them may multiply unforeseeable effects many times over. When palliatives prove to be ineffective, humanity will be forced to devise and implement complex systems for predicting and preventing harmful repercussions on its well-being. As the ecosystem closes in on itself, the mastery and control of such systemic effects will become a basic condition for survival.

Growing awareness of ecological problems should help us to figure out preventive and curative measures with regard to the economic, social, and cultural effects of the global system. That system has taken shape over the course of several centuries, leading first to the industrialization of its center and then to the colonization of its periphery.

We must make no mistake about the scope of the problem. The global system is not limited to capitalism or its ultimate achievement, imperialism; nor is socialism a magic solution to be invoked suddenly as a panacea. The competition or contradiction between socialism and liberal capitalism is rooted in the whole problem lying at the center of the system. If the contradictions of the center are reproduced throughout the system, then an interpretation of the whole system in terms of those contradictions is liable to conceal the effects of the center on the periphery. The middle-term task facing humanity is that of correcting or preventing the destructuring effects of the dominant industrialized societies on their dependent societies. Whether they choose to be socialist or to play the game of liberal capitalism, the underdeveloped countries are prey to the effects of industrialization as it has actually taken shape.

There may be subtle ideological or attitudinal nuances in the relationships between industrialized nations—socialist or capitalist—and the underdeveloped countries. But that does not effect any great change in the mechanisms of domination and their destructuring effects on society. Good intentions, lofty talk, and analyses that are less than serious do not change reality very much. When societies are controlled from the outside, whether the intervention be based on Christian, Marxist, or liberal postulates, they end up being dispossessed of the ability to maintain themselves as societies. In this area nothing could be more hazardous than relying on impressions, desires, or dreams, however worthy may be the aspirations inspiring their proponents.

If one wishes to truly gauge the measure of the collective task facing humanity, then it is the industrial system as such that must be subjected to rigorous critical analysis. I am not suggesting that we should return to the spinning wheel. Gandhi chose that symbol because he was aware of the role that the British textile industry had played in causing the underdevelopment of India and other countries. It is not industrialization that is in question but rather the kind of relationships that have been established between industrial labor and the whole ensemble of activities that enable human beings to produce the necessities of life.

The unequal relationships established between the entrepreneurs who furnish capital and the workers who are reduced to selling or leasing their labor have not at all been transformed into acceptable relationships of complementarity. This is true even when capital is under state control. But that problem is not to be equated with the problem of the relationship between industrial labor on the one hand and the initial labor needed to exploit or give value to basic natural resources. That primary labor is still the labor on which the vast majority of humankind depends for survival.

There is a basic supposition underlying the industrial revolution and the industrial age. Like many basic suppositions, it is accepted unconsciously and taken for granted. It is that only the transformation of resources into commodities gives them value. Raw materials, energy sources, and agricultural products have no real value in themselves. They are simply there to be gathered or dug up. They are raw data.

Before the industrial age, higher value and remuneration went to the marketing and distribution of available goods than to their collection or "production." But when mass production for the market entered the picture, the activities of transformation and commercialization took up such an important place in societal life that primary activities were devalued all the more. The process went on and on as the various activities of transformation became increasingly complex. The share of the raw matter in the value of the finished product grew less as that of the processes of transformation and innovation grew greater. In the end the primary matter hardly enters into the determination of the final price. That price reflects the economic and symbolic value of the commodity designed for consumption or use, and research and development become the prioritized sphere of activity.

That process of evolution bears witness to humanity's progressive mastery of nature and the artificialization of its relationship with its environment. It is so taken for granted that the shift of the working population from the primary sector to secondary, tertiary, and quaternary sectors has become an uncontested index of development.

The inevitable consequence has been the deterioration of exchange rates, to the detriment of those groups and regions that supply primary products. "Added value" is the index of efficiency and hence of social status. Even when the process goes to extremes bordering on the absurd, it is still taken for granted. Thus the box or container holding a "natural product" acquires more value than the product itself, a bottle of water costs more than a bottle of milk, and tomato juice is worth less than its packaging process. The gap between the production of necessities and their consumption becomes so great that it cannot be bridged by the vast majority of human beings. Can it be true, as many claim, that this vast extension of the role of production is a clear sign of the progress that humanity has achieved in the creation of its basic living conditions?

The certitudes of the industrial system had become so unshakable that it took the oil war to make a dent in them. Here again we must not indulge in illusions. The rise in the price of oil was needed to encourage the exploration and exploitation of new energy sources. Thus it dovetailed with the interests of those industries that command the highest added values.

In 1973 the nonaligned nations met in Algiers. They and other Third World nations decided to regain control as a group over their natural resources and the initial stages of their transformation for consumption or use. This decision represented a first attempt to call into question the certitudes and structures of the worldwide industrial system. Even if it has not been very effective, it marked a first step in the transformation of the whole system. And such a transformation will prove obligatory in the end.

Wheat was soon turned to as a possible weapon for counterattack in the oil war. It could cause a heightening of international tensions and be used to blackmail whole peoples for their very survival. But it could also induce many persons to undertake the reflection and action required if the ensemble of human activities is to be reorganized to serve the primary and inescapable objective: meeting the needs of all. Even more necessary than the redeployment of those activities is their reorientation. The very aim and purpose of the system is what must be reexamined. Those in danger of starving to death will force that issue in the end.

Considered from the standpoint of the poor nations, the appropriation of an ever-increasing share of resources and activities for the purpose of arms production, as if this were the basic necessity, makes one wonder whether humanity is not sinking into utter madness.

This aberration of the global system is not yet obvious enough, however, to force a change in the situation. It is not yet certain that we will make the move to a truly humane history where war will no longer be the only way to settle unnegotiated contradictions.

The collective autonomy of the Third World, organizing itself on the fringes of the global system to develop itself and satisfy the basic needs of its populations, remains little more than a working hypothesis. The process of implementing it may have to get under way for humanity to come to realize what has to be done—namely, transform the entire system of industrialization and of the international exchange of goods and services.

At this juncture in history it is undoubtedly the poor, those who have nothing to lose, who will make the decision—once the powerful who rule the world have proved their impotence.

Thesis 10: Education of public opinion in the industrialized nations is a necessary condition for the transformation of the global system.

So long as those in the industrialized nations entertain the shared certainty that their "development" is the necessary model for any and all possible development, the majority of humankind will not be able to set its feet on the road to development. International courtesy may prompt some to continue to call them "developing" nations; but in fact they will remain mired in underdevelopment.

Consider how difficult it has been for the United States to choose to implement a policy of limiting its energy consumption. The difficulty is a particularly pointed indication of the transformation that must take place in outlooks, mental structures, and collective certitudes. Everyone knows that the extension of the American model to humanity as a whole is unthinkable. The whole world is beginning to realize that coexistence between an elite that squanders scarce resources and a majority that lacks basic necessities is untenable in the long run. But these realizations have not sufficed to effect responsible management of available resources, despite the growing awareness that they are not inexhaustible.

The certitudes underlying the industrial system remain to be dismantled. Only then will there be widespread appreciation of the fact that resources found in nature have value in themselves. Industrial labor is not a work of creation in any real sense. However little the raw material may figure in the value of a finished product, it remains a necessity: humanity does not create its products *ex nihilo*. It will always be obliged to transform something given, and that something is not inexhaustible. The efforts of "primitive" humanity to conserve and reproduce its food sources remain exemplary for us. The efforts being made to protect rare species and thus safeguard the diversity of the environment are a step in that direction.

The work that humanity must perform on itself to fit itself for living on "spaceship earth" is as complicated and demanding as that required for the exploration of extraterrestrial space. It must dole out its provisions proportionately, transform and recycle all that can be so dealt with, and avoid all waste. It must learn to administer its patrimony. It took millions of centuries to accumulate that patrimony; if it is abused much longer, the plight of future generations will be at stake. We need to know nature better if we are to use it in a reasonable way.

The need for another kind of development is beginning to be felt everywhere. As yet it is only an intuition, which could easily be turned into a slogan without any solid content. To elaborate its content we must encourage investigation into new energy sources, agricultural methods that do not consume more energy than they produce, and—most importantly—modes of consumption that do not destroy a fragile nature. In this context the new awareness of the dangers of pollution, and of the absurdity of war and overkill, represents an opportunity for humankind. It is beginning to sense that it must discipline itself in order to survive.

Those already dying from the effects of collective life as presently organized will undoubtedly be the ones to teach those benefiting from the present setup that our whole way of life must be changed; that all must have a fair share in the pool of available or potentially available resources and products. The work of shaping or conscientizing public opinion in the industrialized countries is already in progress. Representatives of the Third World have spoken of poverty as the wealth of peoples (Tevoedjré), and the Vatican observer to the International Labor Organization has praised the Chinese model of development in poverty. In affluent societies there are those who reject the present model. This effort must be generalized, however, if access to an affluence long unimaginable is not to become the sole reason for living among those who attain it. The "right of abuse" accorded to proprietors by Roman law cannot be regarded as legitimate.

With the inevitable "redeployment" of industrial activities, be it in the establishment of a new international economic order or in the anarchic implementation of initiatives by groups in control of the economy, the idea must come across that everyone in the world has a stake in the organization of an interdependent planet. This idea must be the focal point of efforts to conscientize the inhabitants of the industrialized countries.

In the short run, the conflict of interests between the industrialized and the underdeveloped nations is what will impress itself on the public mind. There will be more and more crises with regard to employment and competition. Retraining workers for employment new to them will be all the more problematic insofar as it will not have been foreseen and preplanned. Stopgap and protectionist measures will multiply, serving only to conceal the real issues and retard their solution. Societies will become increasingly conservative, and security measures will easily win general approval.

In the long run, however, it is obvious that humanity has a stake in managing its interdependence properly. Short-term conflicts of interest prove to be complementary in the long term. Whatever ways might be devised to ensure an equitable division of labor, it becomes obvious where the solution to the problems of every human group lies. It lies in organizing our world society, not in the self-centered defense of vested rights.

The conscientization of the populace in the industrialized nations must increasingly focus around this shift in perspective. The obviousness of short-term conflicts of interest must give way to the obviousness of their long-term complementarity. If that shift is to take place voluntarily, then public opinion must be accompanied and guided by organizations capable of providing the needed analyses.

This work of conscientization must be carried out against the resistance of commonly accepted ideas and demagoguery in all its forms. It is bound up with the violence that a society must do to itself in order to impose the constraints and obligations that are absolutely necessary. Control of that violence falls within the province of public authorities. They must be delegated the authority they need to impose needed disciplines. They must be able to explain and make credible the measures that strict analysis enjoins as brakes on the spontaneity of conflicting social groups. This presupposes that such conflicts and contradictions will be equitably negotiated.

Societies that attain ease and comfort will be open to interdependence with the rest of humanity only insofar as they become less inegalitarian. Societies that go furthest in redistributing their revenues will probably be the ones most readily inclined to implement real international solidarity. Reciprocity will have every chance to be tested and confirmed. The societal conscience is alert enough to equity that the cost of a more equitable organization of the world will be shared among social groups and not fall solely on the poor and defenseless.

Considering, however, the nature of the electoral process and its concomitant demagoguery in democracies, we must not expect too much from public authorities and groups preoccupied with winning power. We should not assume that they will in fact undertake the analytic and pedagogic work needed to make changes feasible. Voluntary and activist organizations must spring up to link conscientized persons in those nations with their partners in the Third World. They can then work together to clarify and inculcate the new ideas on which the construction of a world society will depend.

Such groups are already at work, of course, animated by a keen sense of worldwide human solidarity or by a results-oriented sense of altruism. These groups must intensify their theoretical and analytical efforts. Otherwise they will continue to be regarded as dreamy idealists by the "realists" who make history or let it happen.

It goes without saying that the church, whose audience and credibility are more solid and real than even it may think, has a role to play in this task. For the task comes down to doing the truth. In the absence of other organizations sufficiently equipped or mobilized for that task, it will be called upon more and more to spotlight the changes in which humanity is involved.

The church's involvement in this task will entail collaboration with all human beings of good will, whether they be organized or not. We will find a paradoxical situation, as is true in the defense of violated human rights: church members will join lay organizations, and persons who are not members of the church will have no problem working with church organizations seeking to gear public opinion toward changing the world.

There is no doubt that Third World proponents will find ecclesiastical channels the easiest way to inform and shape public opinion in the industrialized nations regarding the needed reorganization of the world and what it entails.

It is thus that the political will to change the world will take on shape, consistency, and force—a political will not yet in existence.

What we are looking for is a real counterforce to the force of economic power. Otherwise economic power will make history on the basis of economic calculations alone, leaving governments to pass the social palliatives needed to "adapt" their peoples to their implacable computers and their mathematical decisions affecting everyone.

It is not simply a matter of stirring up the right sentiments in public opinion. What are at stake here are the long-term interests of all. The future of all will depend on a system of international relationships organized to achieve a different sort of development for all. Raising the consciousness of persons in the industrialized nations must be geared toward the implementation and completion of that task.

Chapter 3

Societies Structured and Sacralized in Terms of Inequality

Faced with the necessity of voluntarily fashioning a whole new set of relationships between nations and human groups, we are led to examine the obvious workings and regularities of social dynamics.

What do observation and analysis tell us? It seems clear that human societies, so long as they do not organize to overcome inertia, are structured on the basis of inequality; and they tend to sacralize those structures so that they may be taken for granted and run smoothly.

These two laws of social dynamics must be made clear to all if we are to undertake the task of voluntarily fashioning a new international economic order.

Thesis 11: Left to their own inertia, societies come to be structured in terms of inequality.

It was in the 1960s that public opinion in the industrialized countries began to discern the reality of underdevelopment and the need for action to change the situation. The first major stimulus was the worldwide campaign against hunger launched by the Food and Agricultural Organization of the United Nations. Its purpose was to provide food for peoples who for various reasons could not produce or procure their basic nutritional needs. Direct food subsidies and help in food production were to be the tactics.

The first phase involved the shipment of food surpluses to countries afflicted with endemic famine. Gradually it was realized that the fight against hunger was really a fight for development. Technical cooperation and the transfer of know-how entered the picture. The hope was that the technological gap between developed and underdeveloped nations could be closed. As time went on, however, it became obvious that the disparities between rich and poor were growing, not only on the international front but also in the underdeveloped countries themselves. The rich were getting richer, and the poor were getting poorer.

Deterioration in the exchange rate between providers of primary products and producers of manufactured products then appeared as the evil to be combated; but the root of the problem was not uncovered. Price stabilization in contracts

34

became the object of international negotiations, but truly effective accords were hard to come by. Progress on that front will come only when the underlying problem is posed clearly.

Deterioration in exchange rates flows of necessity from the industrialization of societies. So long as added value is the only thing that matters, the value of primary products is bound to diminish both relatively and absolutely, particularly insofar as the absolute value of commodities is measurable only in terms of the world market. The higher the cost of product transformation, research, and innovation, the greater will be the relative decline in the share and purchasing power of those who provide primary products. Left to itself, this logic is implacable. Equally inevitable is the shift of the working population to situations and jobs that will afford readier access to available goods.

International relationships are not the only area where the structuring of human groups in terms of inequality is evident. It is in the dynamics of societal life that such structuring seems to be part of the very nature of things, like inertia or gravity. Left to the mercy of the forces at work, societies tend toward inequality, just as rivers flow toward the ocean.

In order to understand this inertia, we must take into account the irreducible asymmetry of human relationships. When the effects of that inertia become obvious, they affront the ethical sensibility or instinct of most persons. Injustice appears indefensible, even to those who do not dream of any utopian or mythical egalitarianism. But the parent is not the child: their relationship is asymmetrical. Male is not female. Someone who comes from a long line of entrepreneurs does not start life with the same chances as someone who comes from a family of small investors who have suffered the effects of monetary erosion. Even before that, one's genetic heritage accounts for certain irradicable inequalities. Education and opportunity give some the chance that others will go without. In the competition for survival and social success, inequities and handicaps are there from the very beginning. Equal opportunity, so highly vaunted in U.S. society, holds true only for the strongest, the most skilful, and those who have the least scruples about seizing any means to success.

Persons who have a sense of justice and who have not had a fair chance might well give way to despair if exceptions to this general rule were not observable. Leaving aside projections of future classless societies, we do find relatively egalitarian societies in the world. At least we find societies that are egalitarian enough to ensure that their poor have not been disregarded and deprived of basic necessities.

This is generally the case in traditional societies where destructuring has not gone far enough to be noticeable. Strict laws governing work activities or the distribution of resources prevent a drifting toward excessive inequality, even though some may be richer than others because of kinship or their management of goods. Socially and mentally the traditional group is generally structured in such a way as to penalize and rectify inequality when it goes beyond the tolerance point. Ethnologists talk glibly about "jealousy" or "envy" when they refer to this keen sense of equality; superficial observers see only a tendency toward leveling and mediocrity.

A more profound analysis suggests that the relative equality of such societies is the result of voluntary strategies for regulating social relationships. Those strategies are generally based on inherited norms that have been at work for ages to rule out excessive or intolerable differences. Individuals and groups are aligned in such a way as to make standing out or setting oneself apart unacceptable or impossible. In peasant societies such behavior is regarded with condescension or disdain. This attitude is both the effect and the reverse side of their efforts to regulate the inertial tendencies toward inequality. The egalitarianism imposed in such societies, to which all adhere by choice or by constraint, is an attitude or a pattern of behavior built up over centuries through the implementation of procedures to regulate societal dynamics.

Although such societies may not be exemplary in every respect, especially inasmuch as they generally suffer from the processes of destructuration and sclerosis, their practices do suggest how we might reduce intolerable forms of inequality.

In taking note of the inevitability of inequality in the structuring of societies, and of the exception embodied in traditional societies, one realizes more clearly what is at issue here. It is not the projection or realization of egalitarian dreams or utopias. Instead it is a matter of organizing and implementing practices that will pose resistance to the inevitable thrust toward inequality. In this area as in others, the transition from dream to reality does not come about from a desperate effort to realize a dream, but rather from slow, persistent work on reality to impose on it a regulated system of norms and sanctions. Such work is undoubtedly less entrancing than the projection of an imagined future very different from the present. It has a better chance of being effective if it is sustained and imposed by the collective will.

To view the inertial drift of societies toward inequality as a hard-and-fast law is to bind oneself to a voluntarist viewpoint as impossible and yet necessary as the effort to keep something heavier than air up in the air. The problem must be solved collectively, which presupposes a colossal effort of conscientization and imagination. Otherwise humanity will not cross the threshold standing before it, the threshold on which its future depends.

Such an approach to a world policy is often reproachfully labelled "reformism." But that reproach is no more tenable than other stereotypes offered in place of serious thinking. The era of utopian, messianic, or "scientific" revolutions is drawing to a close. Humanity will not shape itself by submitting to laws or determinisms of either nature or human history. Instead it must actively resist them, organizing itself to master and transcend them. The willed construction of societies is as impossible and as necessary as aeronautics and astronautics. It was thought that the human being was the only obstacle to space progress before we learned how to overcome the shock of rocket acceleration. Now humanity will have to learn how to transcend itself again, once the failure of "liberal" or state-sponsored policies makes that necessity clear.

The task will seem impossible only so long as humanity does not make the decision to undertake it collectively, with all the tenacity and perseverance required to implement mechanisms and structures designed to regulate relationships between social groups and nations.

When representatives of the Third World propose the establishment of a new international economic order, they are talking about the construction of partnership liaisons. The fact that their efforts have not met with success does not mean that the issue is a false one. Sooner or later humanity will have to get down to regulating and controlling a situation of inequality that has become intolerable even to the privileged.

In the long run we shall be forced to adopt a strategy designed to organize resistance to the inevitable slide of societies toward inequality. That resistance will have to be active, adroit, arbitrary, political, and cultural. Its procedures will necessarily be complicated, but they can be thought out and mastered. The real problem is the political will needed to get the process going.

Thesis 12: Societies fashion gods for themselves, and those gods become their masters.

Societies must impose the constraints they need in order to function. The sacralization of those obligations seems to be a precondition for imposing them and making their relevance clear. If they are to work automatically, they must seem so self-evident that no one would think of changing them.

Human beings establish a relationship with what they regard as the realm of the sacred by recognizing and establishing certain things as being outside their control and mastery. Certain realities, representation, and values impose themselves on human beings. What is considered sacred (life, parenthood, country, deities, etc.) becomes indisputable and untouchable.

But relationships with the sacred, like all human relationships, are fashioned and reproduced through complex sequences of attitudes, representations, and procedures. Hence they must be analyzed over and over again, unless their explanation is thought to lie in an appeal to some religious instinct inherent in human nature. If human beings exist only insofar as they individually and collectively fashion themselves, winning their humanity from nature, then I am inclined to think that they do not fashion their gods "instinctively" as an animal defines and organizes its territory. And this is true even though the human practice is so widespread that it seems to flow from the very nature of things.

To interpret such practices as an escape from reality or as the projection of unrealizable dreams into the beyond is not to explain them at all, even though one may thereby categorize them in terms of some overall vision of human behavior. If religion is merely an impotent protest against real misery, then it should be easier than it apparently is to liberate human beings from it in those places where activists seem bent on doing so. But the fact is that deities proliferate in the very societies that want to be godless.

The sacralization of things that escape human mastery seems to be bound up with an effort to establish a manageable relationship with that which escapes human control or human transformation. To define a sacred realm is to provide oneself with the possibility of achieving a relationship to it by recognizing the provisional or definitive limits of human control.

In the long run the sacralization of social norms, structures, and organizations tends to ensure that they will be taken for granted and run as smoothly as they can. This is true whether one sacralizes democracy or tyranny. When something lies beyond debate and discussion, it serves as the very infrastructure of community life. That life becomes real and operative only insofar as it is grounded on ideological certitudes that are so obvious that they become unconscious and hence normative. Thus we find all sorts of symbolic or practical predominances: of the right hand over the left, so that being left-handed is unthinkable; of parent over child, so that knowledge and wisdom can only be transmitted; of male over female, so that their complementarity can only be unilateral; of cleric and monk over lay person, so that the model of Christian living can only be scholarly or eschatological; of king over people, so that power and authority is seen as something delegated by God; and so forth. These attitudes are typical examples of certitudes that are arbitrarily constructed and culturally imposed and that serve as the basis for the functioning of a society. Things that we do not think about determine what we do think about. Those certitudes must be observed and practiced lest societal cohesion be jeopardized.

The divinization of Caesar and the sacred anointing of kings are perfect examples of such sacralizing processes. They force acceptance because experience seems to prove that they work. Such sacralization is all the more operative and effective insofar as it is not called into question. Violation is sacrilege. In a sacralized society that means exclusion not only from society but from the mental universe underlying it. Heretics, schismatics, and atheists cease to exist civilly, even if they are not condemned to physical extermination.

Traditional societies are generally religious or even highly sacralized. The main reason is not that those who exercise knowledge or power over the sacred have simply "manipulated" the people, though that may seem to be obvious in certain cases. The deeper, underlying reason is that those societies have been fashioned in such cohesiveness with the sacred, for so long a time, that the configuration of the society seems to be a divine rather than a human work. It becomes an object of ritual celebration. The idea of dealing with elements that have become irrelevant or inoperative is simply ruled out. In that respect we see the same dynamics at work in widely scattered phenomena: the strict definition of rites and instruments in the old Catholic liturgy, the ritual battles of ancient warriors, and the practices of Masonic lodges.

As long as such institutions continue to function, safe from the intervention of the agents of social dynamics, they have as much value as the most uncontroversial organizations and those that are considered secularized. The problem arises when they become inoperative and hence must be transformed. Then social and political action runs up against forms of resistance that are the most difficult to surmount. Conscientization and negotiation must take place to reinterpret the age-old sacralized heritage so that unfortunate consequences do not ensue for future generations. This holds true whether it is a matter of digging a well where God is assumed to be the Lord of water, distributing church land to rural indigents where such land is regarded as holy ground, or deposing a king where he is regarded as the anointed lieutenant of God.

The history of the post-Christian West is very instructive here. In medieval Christendom the sacralization of social systems was deep-rooted and unquestionable. When those systems had to be changed, it could only be done by the "voluntary" negation of the God who served as their point of reference or keystone. A rationalist approach necessarily ruled out recourse to God as a substitute for, or complement to, research into the laws or mechanisms of nature and society. That did not imply the negation of God, however. The negation was necessary to transform a sacralized society. The post-Christian West has not yet recovered from that step; and the rest of the world is still feeling the backlash of Western society's attempt to settle accounts with itself and with the church that administered its civil religion.

The way that crisis has been handled in fact does not end debate as to how to proceed with inevitable sacralizations and necessary desacralizations. We need only note the proliferation of cults and religious attitudes in those societies most committed to structuring themselves on the basis of scientific analysis. That should make us realize that much work remains to be done if human beings are to be capable of controlling their irrepressible tendency to fabricate gods. The investment of religious feeling in utopian projections or prospects for social change is no less impressive and disquieting. The emotional resistance offered to such analyses or evocations bears witness to their relevance. The dosage of sacredness tends to increase even as sacredness is being denied.

Anyone concerned about furthering the transformation of the global system, either by mobilizing Third World consciousness or calling the certitudes of the First World into question, must be willing to explore individual and societal relationships with the sacred and ways to master them. This is not a minor or marginal aspect of developmental efforts. It is a precondition for implementing processes of development that will have some hope of success in restructuring societies.

The denial of God or gods is as intangible and uncontrollable as divine worship. Here human behavior patterns are shaped in the depths of the unconscious, where reasoning can scarcely reach. To realize with Hamlet that there are more things in heaven and on earth than are dreamed of in our philosophies is not to take refuge in mysteriousness. It simply enables us to get a handle on certain aspects of reality that escape positivistic rationalism but must nevertheless be mastered if we are to lead a truly human existence. We must manage our relationships with the sacred and God; we must interpret them as rigorously as we can. These tasks continue to be of the utmost importance because such relationships continue to be operative even when they are declared to be illusory.

When the sacralization of social or mental structures appears to be an obstacle to development, mere denial of such sacralization will not do. It must instead be reintegrated into the overall picture if we are to progress in our mastery of social dynamics.

Chapter 4

The Role of the Church in the Transformation of the World

It is considered good form to regard the Catholic Church as hopelessly marginalized from societal life, due to the process of secularization. But observation and analysis constrain us to take due notice of the roles proposed for the church, or even imposed on it, in helping to trigger a process of development that will be to the benefit of all.

These contributory roles have to do with uncovering or analyzing the social mechanisms that must be changed to make development possible, and with participating in the collective conscientization involved in that process.

These tasks are not fill-in jobs to be undertaken simply because other organizations are not doing them. They flow from the very mission of the church, which is to proclaim the good news, the word of God.

Thesis 13: The church has a role to play in the transformation of the world.

When we talk about *the church* and the problems of our day, we must realize what we mean. We are not talking about the hierarchy or the ecclesiastical apparatus; nor are we talking about some nebulous "people of God" floating around somewhere. We are talking about the ensemble of those who believe in Jesus Christ and who have organized themselves to lead their lives along the lines prompted by their faith. "Fashioned by the faith and its sacraments," as Thomas Aquinas put it, this church continually builds itself up by hearing and speaking the word of God and by organizing itself hierarchically to carry out its practice accordingly.

As it confronts the problems of a world in the making, the Catholic Church is potentially ecumenical. This is true even though internal contradictions produced by its history may continue to divide it, and even though awareness of the tasks imposed on it and the various ways to tackle them continually threaten to evoke new conflicts within the church. To exist as a church, it simply must participate somehow in the efforts of human beings to fashion a habitable earth.

Existing only there where some gather together in the name of the Lord around a bishop, who symbolizes and realizes that presence, the Catholic

40

Church is an international organization. Hence its participation in the collective life of humanity is never insignificant, whether it chooses to assume its role or not. For better or for worse, the self-image it has fashioned over the centuries accompanies the church, without ever confining it to fixed, stereotyped roles. The church exists socially. Hence it helps willy-nilly to abet or hinder the organization and transformation of relationships between human groups.

To comprehend the church's functioning, then, we must observe and analyze it as we would any other social organization. We should not try to deduce its practices from the church's idea of itself, or from the idea of others as to what it is or ought to be. It is from the church's practice that we may descry the contours of its identity, the main thrust of its inner dynamics. But inasmuch as observation can never be exhaustive, any analysis of the church's actual or potential roles must be framed in terms of a prospective hypothesis—that is, what the church could become at this point, when humanity itself is hesitant about the road to take in building its future.

I intend to say something about the roles proposed to the Catholic Church at this point in history, its competence to assume them, and the dovetailing of those roles with the church's inner dynamics, tradition, and collective memory. My reading of the situation is focused around the reality that the church confronts right now, and what it will mean for the church if it chooses to get involved. Hence I am not going to assert flatly that this is what the church should be or do. I am simply suggesting what the church could do and could become if it takes on the tasks at hand. Appeals are addressed to the church because it does exist and does function, for better or for worse, more than it might seem to many observers.

For some time now, post-Christian societies have been organizing themselves to handle the services that once were the province of the ecclesiastical institution. It is now old hat to say the the church has become marginal in society. And because medieval Christendom was almost the only social construct where Christianity played such a role, it is easily assumed that the present marginality of the church is a worldwide phenomenon. The relative decrease in the number of Christians and, even more obviously, the decrease in the number of those who allow themselves to be guided by the ecclesiastical institution only serve to heighten the impression that the church and Christianity are vanishing historical realities. The same impression is evident within the church, producing either disenchantment or defensive focus on "eternal" principles or traditions. As a result, the performance of services, for which there is less and less personnel, threatens to distract attention from the tasks that are now being proposed to the church, tasks for which other organizations are not prepared.

As one who has closely followed the whole problematic and practice of development over many years, and who has wondered about the needed transformation of social and mental structures, I cannot help but take note of the social demands being made of the church. It is being asked to take charge of various tasks related to the construction of national societies and a world society, tasks for which other social agencies are often unavailable or unprepared.

A social demand for church intervention in the course of history is not confirmed in the same way that the potential market demand for a product or concrete service is. Although we may infer it from observing the relationships between churches and societies, it is more difficult to actually prove it. So I would merely offer this working hypothesis: here and there around the world we find that the church is expected to offer its contribution—helping to investigate problems related to the organization of community life, to seek out solutions, and, perhaps most important of all, to initiate the process of reorganizing relationships between human groups.

On the one hand even Christians no longer look to the church to tell them how they should manage their personal lives, interpersonal relationships, and family or professional responsibilities. But on the other hand even those who do not frequent the church are inclined to think that it may be qualified and somehow obligated to share the task of grasping or guiding the required transformations of the global system affecting all. There is general awareness now of the danger that the church could maintain too tight a grip on the conduct of societies. That sensitivity is evident in the church itself, which has become suspicious of triumphalism. The fact remains, however, that the church is expected to take an active part in reducing inequality, poverty, and injustice, and in exploring steps toward a more satisfactory organization of societal life.

In many instances this desire is prompted by the absence or impotence of other organizations. Societal efforts to work on society are very complicated. Every organization, whether it be a government agency, a labor union, or a political party, finds itself riveted to its own immediate responsibilities. It does not have the time or energy to ponder overall societal issues. Herein lies the role of international organizations, of course. But because they operate on delegated powers, they are often obstructed or neutralized by the conflicts that divide their members. It may well be that within international organizations there is the greatest desire for the church to shoulder its responsibilities. What they expect most, perhaps, is that the church will make clear what exactly is at stake in the present situation, as we confront a world in need of transformation.

The Catholic Church has an international dimension by virtue of its real or potential transconfessionality. It constitutes a socio-cultural locale in which various persons, who disagree with each other on the best way to reorganize the planet, have an additional chance to communicate with each other and reach agreement on the pathways to be explored in fashioning a new international order.

This societal expectation, however vague, is clearly discernible. And it coincides with yearnings and movements at work within the church. The church has gradually assimilated criticisms of its role in the past. It now realizes that it cannot accept or side with a way of organizing the world that results in underdevelopment, injustice, and poverty for the vast majority of humankind.

There has been critical analysis of what the church has sacralized in the past, and a return to its sources has forced it to explore afresh its own collective memory. Thus it has gradually discovered, or rediscovered, that love—charity—is its unique law. And charity does not mean almsgiving devoid of involvement in efforts to overcome the causes of poverty. It takes on a political cast insofar as we realize that authentic worship of God means permitting every human being to forge an existence in the image and likeness of God.

Sensitivity to injustice and poverty is not simply a matter of noble sentiments, which can produce little more than edifying talk. It is something at work in the ecclesial body, impelling some to become poor alongside the poor and others to become guerrilla fighters alongside other guerrilla fighters. To be sure, many of them abandon the ecclesiastical institution, because they despair of seeing transformations in it. Nevertheless they remain in unseen solidarity with those inside the church who share their struggle for conversion to what is essential and who work in its behalf. Thus they help promote the tasks that must be performed if we are to reshape the world.

This convergence between demand and ecclesial response to it is one of the most astonishing phenomena in church history. It might seem nothing more than a mirage, and the church itself has sometimes not been aware of it. But it is a fact and a sign of the time. There are inertial factors and countervailing forces within the church, to be sure. In the last analysis, however, they have little weight against the historical thrust that Christianity has never ceased to be, even when it seemed to harden into a set of totalitarian aims or practices.

When Christianity denied the divinity of Caesar, it anticipated the hopes of the poor who had been condemned to perpetual bondage by the prevailing system. Even centuries of institutional and political perversion could not snuff out that creative élan. Though it may not have had any explicitly political aim, Christianity was a factor in the desacralization of the ancient social organization and hence in its transformation.

Spurred by concern over its identity and social function, the church today is more attentive to the course of world history and the signs of the time. To that extent it is also open to the new tasks facing humankind, as it comes to realize that those tasks coincide with its own mission.

Thesis 14: The church has a role to play in the liberation of peoples it has long induced or constrained to resignation.

Various human groups are turning to the church because they do not know where else to turn. One significant grouping is that of the peoples in underdeveloped countries whom the church helped to incorporate into the global system as dependents. These are the little "Christendoms," modeled after medieval Christendom, that have been in existence since the fifteenth century. The Catholic Church was authorized to evangelize certain populations while their European conquerors colonized them, exploited them, and sometimes exterminated them. The church made every effort to lead them to heaven, preaching resignation to the brutal conditions imposed on them here on earth.

To be sure, there were many defenders of the poor and oppressed among the missionaries who lived during that era of church expansion. The most famous of them, Bartolomé de Las Casas, was an ardent defender of the Amerindians. He helped to foster the study of international law and human rights. He stands for many other missionaries who were truly in fellowship with the oppressed, even though their pastoral and catechetical activity helped to keep the system of domination running smoothly. In various parts of the Philippines and the Americas the priest is still viewed with respect and tender regard because the indigenous peoples have a long memory. They know that the missionaries were on their side through it all, even when they could not defend them.

But the fact remains that the ecclesiastical institution helped to inculcate submission to the authority of the powerful. It sacralized resignation to the will of God as a necessary manifestation of true religion. It helped to destructure local societies by desecrating the native religions that had legitimated them. Thus it was of great help to the agents of colonization, which could go to the extreme of ethnocide. When we reflect on the role of the church in the development of peoples, we certainly cannot conceal or pass over in silence this perversion of Christianity. And we must admit that it often marked the efforts of the most unselfish and generous preachers of the gospel message. Their intentions are not in question. But their good intentions did not change the effects of enforced acculturation, which is at the root of the passivity and fatalism evident among peoples deprived of control over their societal life.

In the geopolitical atmosphere thus created, the church found itself in charge of the religious life of entire populations, not to mention the educational and social services for which it was responsible. Endowed with ideological power and authority that ensure the trust or submission of entire peoples, the church now holds one of the keys to the social changes demanded by the times. Governments, which often pay more attention to the international scene, are not mistaken in trying to win legitimation from the church. Often closely allied to successive systems of domination in past centuries, the church now finds itself caught between two alternatives. It can either continue to sacralize the established order, even if that order maintains itself through terror, or it can apply its energy and its following to the liberation of the poor.

The way in which local churches move beyond their present indecision will have profound implications for the future of the universal church. It will be of even more decisive importance for the future of those peoples now held in a state of dependence. Militant factions in those countries may opt for liberation without worrying about the course of the church, following the lead of protest movements against the church in post-Christian societies. But the conscientization and mobilization of the masses will depend in large measure on attitudes and strategies formulated within the church.

Inasmuch as it helped to sacralize resignation, the ecclesiastical institution is the only one that can desacralize that attitude. Only it can remove the obstacle to change that is posed by the "will of God," which has been used to inculcate submission to those in authority as if they were God's lieutenants. Insofar as God is recognized as God, things imposed in God's name can be dismantled only with the encouragement and approval of those delegated to speak on God's behalf.

If the church finds itself at the very heart of the contradictions plaguing societies undergoing change, if it is involved in their fissures and fixations, it is because the church has been in charge of their relationship with God. That relationship is never insignificant. In many countries the inertial stance of the institutional church tends to legitimate the powers in place, even though it may seek to correct their excesses. Long-term observation suggests, however, that we must also consider responsible, meaningful church practices that tend to legitimate ruptures with the status quo, ruptures that must take place if there is to be change.

The unthinkable becomes thinkable when the church, which had been preaching resignation, begins to tell the poor that it is God who is summoning them to stand on their own two feet; that it is God who wants them to take in hand the work of building the social organizations they need to improve their living conditions. We then have the possibility of a conscientization process very different from the one that has to be implemented if it is done in spite of the church. The latter may entail a backlash of guilt feelings, because the church's claim to speak in God's name may not be denied even by those who will no longer submit to church tutelage.

Mass movements of the first type often begin with the establishment of basic ecclesial communities in which members try to rediscover the good news proclaimed to the poor. They share the exhilaration of the exodus from Egypt or the return of the Jews from exile. Even in the midst of repression they feel themselves to be a captive people in the process of liberating itself. Calmly and peacefully they go about the process, having no weapon but the gospel message and its subversive, mobilizing force.

It is not by chance that a theology of liberation began to take shape in such a context. Far from being a messianic testimonial on the necessity of revolution, that theology has taken shape as the language of a people moving out onto the road to liberation and discovering God's self-revelation as liberator. The role proposed to the church is that of organizing and mobilizing the resources at its disposal in order to conscientize those who are ready to listen to what it has to say. In many instances only the church has access to them.

Such groups may ask the church to do nothing more than ritualize or canonize the celebrations that enable them to survive in their misery and impotence. But we should not let that blind us to the fact that they are ready to be turned to new pathways once they are shown that such pathways are open to them. Because they have confidence in the church, they are ready to follow it once it explains the real import of its change of policy and the measures it proposes to them. To move from legitimating the established order to legitimating a revolution is a radical change for the church, a process of conversion leading it back to its original dynamics. It cannot be lived collectively without some ambiguity and some excesses of spiritual exhilaration. But that should not thwart the process itself, which is bound to meet with resistance and rejection in some quarters.

Under the influence of centuries of submissiveness to a "divine order" of things, those involved in such a conversion process—leaders and followers— must restructure their thought patterns and their certitudes. They may well suffer fear and trembling at times. That will surprise only those who do not know from experience how deep loyalty to the church can be—for better or for worse—in those who place their trust in it.

Local churches, called upon to help conscientize the peoples they have educated to submissiveness, can shoulder the tasks that they see to be necessary and urgent. But if this is to happen, the universal church must be capable of appreciating what is at stake in the changes. It is nothing less than the future of now dependent peoples and the relevance to them of the gospel message that has been entrusted to the church.

The fear that often paralyzes church members and its institutional apparatus is certainly understandable. The potential explosions are awesome to contemplate. Yet the ravages of unconquered fear are even more dangerous. If the church is not bold enough to shoulder certain tasks, no one else will be there to shoulder them. Underdevelopment will continue to wreak poverty and dehumanization on countless human beings. If it is indeed true that the blood of martyrs is the seedbed of Christianity, then we may take hope from the blood of those who are being killed because they took seriously the demands of the gospel and energetically proclaimed it to the poor. The church must wake up from its slumber in the shade of the princely palaces of this world.

Today millions of Christians are to be found in countries that were held under colonial and postcolonial domination for centuries. As they organize and mobilize to change the world, a world in which they and their fellow human beings have less and less influence, the whole church finds itself on the move. It is being asked to help make possible the changes once thought impossible.

It is in the church that the cry of the voiceless oppressed has the best chance of being heard. Even though the churched are inclined to say only what is supposed to be said, the voice of the poor finds an echo when they dare to express themselves. Its reverberations cannot be stifled completely, no matter how rigid structures become. Even if it is grounded on nothing more than "noble sentiments," the sensitivity of Christians to the cry of the oppressed can have unforeseen effects.

Thesis 15: The church has a role to play in the conscientization of peoples compelled to reinterpret their traditional religions.

The church will sometimes find itself present, if only marginally, to a people whose religion has come down to them from the distant past—either as their traditional religion or as an imported religion that was interiorized long ago. Conversions to Christianity may be taking place or there may be local efforts afoot to dialogue with the church and its message. When such a situation exists, the church certainly has a role to play. It must help those peoples to reinterpret their religious traditions insofar as it is necessary when they confront new situations created by outside intervention.

Having arrived with merchants, soldiers, or colonists, whether in collusion or competition with them, the church willy-nilly played a role in disturbing the local religious traditions and structures. It was a part of the civilization that imposed itself on another people by virtue of its power. The technological and cultural innovations of the dominant society called into question inherited mental and religious structures. The meaningfulness and relevance of those inherited structures could no longer be taken for granted. The ordered arrangement of myths, rites, beliefs, and symbols was disrupted, along with the cohesiveness they ensured. At the same time the social representations, norms, and systemizations of the foreign society concealed authentic Christian tenets not directly perceptible. As a result the church frequently seemed at first glance to be linked up with "unbelief." And indeed it was unbelief when the church, failing to take due note of indigenous traditions and practices, unwittingly helped to destroy them or render them meaningless.

Here, then, the church has a duty to perform. By paying respectful attention to traditional attitudes and mores, and by trying to understand them, the church must help peoples to envision the possible perdurance of their religious life amid the societal upheavals that they can do so little to control. The church must try to point up the contradictions between the collective behavior patterns of the dominant society and the message entrusted to the care of the church. This can mark a first breach in the systems of seemingly self-evident certitudes that must eventually be dismantled.

The first Christians were viewed as atheists in the Roman Empire. Indeed this was their strength vis-à-vis a social organization whose sacralizations were already crumbling. That process has reoccurred more often than we may think. Missionaries have often failed to take cognizance of the image that the missionized were forming of them. Being on the side of the conquerors, they could not perceive the identification being made between the secularizing action of their own society on the one hand and the religion they were propagating on the other. Even when their currency did not bear the inscription "In God We Trust," their patterns of thought and action could not help but appear to be those of their religion as well. The profanation of springs and sacred woods, the disruption of cultic places and times, and other such actions could hardly be viewed as manifestations of worship "in spirit and in truth." Most of the time what came across was an air and attitude of impiety.

Even if the church resists the perversions and consequences of the civilization it is propagating, it cannot distinguish itself from that civilization except by making every effort to comprehend the inner nature of the religious beliefs and practices of a non-Christian people. It cannot approach others with the condescension of one who possesses the standard for all true religion. Instead it must exercise the intelligence required to grasp what others are experiencing when they prostrate themselves before what they regard as sacred. It will take even more time for the church to get over the idea of approaching other religions in order to find in them stepping stones to the fulness it alone possesses, though that attitude does mark a first step toward respecting the mystery of "the other."

The disruption of traditional religions alive in underdeveloped societies would not be so devastating as it often is if another factor were not at work. As their native certitudes crumble, their hermeneutic ability is also deeply affected. Their ability to reinterpret and reconstruct their systems of the represenations and norms that give meaning to their lives is seriously impaired. What was once taken for granted becomes unthinkable. The symbolic function itself is blocked, because there is no possibility for the "theological" work required to analyze past traditions and gain a new understanding of their meaning.

Consider the farmers who refuse to dig the irrigation ditches needed in dry seasons because such a practice seems to them a sacrilegious encroachment on a domain reserved to God. They do not deserve the condescension or disdain they are likely to run up against. What they need, rather, is time to reflect on their representation of God, a process of apprenticeship in which respect is shown for their certitudes. This will enable them to change their universe, to "negotiate" their relationship with God and establish it anew. From submission to a jealous, omnipotent God they will then be able to move on to active collaboration with God, the creator of creators. Most of the time, however, such a process of negotiation is not even possible. Either the pace of socio-cultural change is too fast, or very few of those who speak for God are prepared for such processes of apprenticeship.

To be sure, the problems are rarely posed in such crystal-clear terms. Generally speaking, however, we can say that little thought is given to the whole matter. Societies can be unhinged when doubts are cast on their representations of the sacred or their relationships to it. But those who conceive and implement development policies rarely concern themselves with that issue.

It is the church's role to pay heed to this dimension of societal change. In the task of conscientization it must assume responsibility for nurturing the attitudes, convictions, and procedures that will enable persons to envision the changes that are now necessary, without totally nullifying what they once took for granted.

In this area missiological reflection and missionary practice have been ahead of the theory and practice of development. Missionaries have long realized that the proclamation of the gospel message and the organization of societal life around it can be effective and authentic only when envisioned in terms of a graft or a seed. If the message is to be welcomed in such a way that it reorganizes the whole life of those who receive it, then it must be assimilated, interiorized, and truly appropriated by them. It must reinterpret their heritage for them, without destroying that heritage.

Discretion and attentiveness, then, are part of the process, at least in theory. With them conscientization is enriched. Starting with what a group of persons knows and can assimilate, it can enable them to enrich their heritage without breaking totally away from the past and thereby losing all trace of their own cultural creativity.

Thus the church is one of the few organizations qualified to perform certain tasks for peoples striving for self-determination. Those tasks may have to do with peoples who have accepted its message and now seek to be integrated into its constituent communities. Or they may have to do with peoples among whom the church has established itself merely to offer silent witness to the God it adores.

In the long run, even when the damage done to native religious traditions and their cohesiveness seems irreparable, the presence of the church can be useful when it is open to constructive dialogue. It can help those peoples to rediscover their soul and thus take the first step toward regaining mastery over their own social dynamics.

There have been may forms of more or less successful syncretism, ranging from voodoo to popular Catholicism in all its varieties. They bear witness to the long-term work that peoples can accomplish by themselves. This "underground" work may disconcert the champions of orthodoxy and "informed religion." Nevertheless it is necessary for the transformation of religious life, and hence social life, without traumatic ruptures.

For centuries the church has been in conflict with societies desacralized in reaction to its ideological power and authority. This has hardly prepared the church to negotiate integrative religious transformations. It has, however, forced the church to reinterpret the relationships between religion and social life in societies that were undergoing secularization. That may incline the church to appreciate and make clear the interpretive work that must be done if societies are not to be totally unhinged when their religious life is shaken by inescapable social transformations.

And what is the mission of the church among those who have joined its communities and put their trust in it? The church must help them to deal with the sweeping changes it has partly provoked by preaching the gospel message. Consider the elderly African bishop who admitted he had spent his whole adult life opposing revivals of his traditional religion, only to realize belatedly that the God of Jesus Christ was none other than the God of his forefathers. That was his way of expressing the continuity-in-discontinuity that is the key to mastering such mutations. Or take the case of the priest in India who devotes his efforts to a christological interpretation of the Vedic texts, not to force them into some apologetic mold but to understand them himself on the basis of his Indian and Christian background. He is on the same road, taking the risk of upsetting both his Christian and Indian brothers and sisters. Many persons active in the pastoral ministry of the church, who share the lives of their peoples and seek to heighten their consciousness, are fully aware of the complexity and gravity of the task.

There is no reason why there should not be progress in the praxis of a conscientization that takes into account the religious dimension of changes required in societies undergoing destructuring. There should also be progress in our reflection on that praxis. If these gains are made, we can win much time and energy for both development and evangelization, particularly in the case of peoples who are open to the message and perspectives offered them by the church. Here we clearly have one of the major tasks facing the church if it is to participate in the development of peoples.

Thesis 16: The church has a role to play in the conscientization and education of public opinion in the industrialized countries, on which the needed transformation of the global system depends to a large extent.

Collective awareness in so-called advanced societies is heavily influenced by the conviction that they are indeed in advance of underdeveloped societies. This is true even though there are now some twinges of doubt about the global meaning and relevance of what is called "progress." Hence the sensitization of public opinion in those countries to the distorted aspects of their "progress" is one of the important preconditions for global change. There is a growing realization, here and there, that a different sort of development is necessary. Many are beginning to wonder about the future of a civilization in crisis, though the whole issue is generally posed in a mythical framework.

The crisis itself, however, has already had a serious impact on employment and the standard of living. This tends to fix attention on advantages already won and make persons anxious about losing them. In such a situation it is even harder for them to envision a worldwide redistribution of resources, production activities, or power. Industrialized societies are being pressured in the direction of a more equitable distribution of income when there is no assurance that it will grow. Thus they are sorely tempted to turn in upon themselves and preserve the affluence they have attained, while still trying to deal with the contradictions posed by unequal access of various social groups to resources that seem to be within the reach of all.

Thus domestic struggles for justice are in danger of impeding the struggle for international justice. That struggle seemed more important when available resources seemed to be subject to unlimited growth.

In such a crisis organizations and associations tend to polarize around their own immediate, legitimate interests. They refuse to ponder long-term action for the transformation of the global system, even though the fate of most human beings will depend on such transformation.

One may be able to prove that in the long run the interests of underdeveloped and of industrialized nations are complementary, that rational organization of their relationships would augment production of the goods needed to satisfy the needs of all. But in the short run it is the clash of interests that seems most obvious to all, particularly to those condemned, by worldwide competition, to unemployment or change to a different kind of employment.

Political, cultural, religious, and labor-union leaders bear a heavy weight of responsibility for causing this situation, which is bound to intensify. They did not foresee—though it was predictable—the backlash effect of worldwide development and modernization policies on their own industrialized nations. They should have undertaken long-term planning for the reconversion processes that would be needed. Now the rebound effect of peripheral destructuring on the industrial heartland is clearly noticeable, analyzable, and inescapable. It is time to tackle the problem in terms of the whole worldwide system. To concentrate energy on controlling social transformations only in the industrialized countries would now be catastrophic for both those nations and the whole world.

Advocates of the just rights of groups whose well-being is threatened find themselves in a bind. The urgency of local situations forces them to focus on short-term problems and current dissatisfactions. Even though some leaders may be aware of the long-range problems confronting societies, they are often impotent in the face of societal and group dynamics. Austerity, even when widely and fairly shared, goes against the shibboleths of demagoguery; and it is hard to see how demagoguery can be completely eliminated from the politics of democracy. Only wartime situations, totalitarian policies, or those temporary phases of great social creativity and openness provide room for the sort of voluntary or forced mobilization needed to pressure societies into adopting the regulations required for mastering their dynamics.

If such a leap is to be possible, societies must be able to entertain it as a possibility. Against the evidence of short-term contradictions, they must be able to see the complementarity of interests in the long run so that present certitudes gradually shift toward those required in the future.

Few organizations or associations are motivated or mobilized for that sort of societal effort, which goes against the grain of current certitudes. It is a prophetic effort, wholly contrary to demagoguery. It is not that the prophet predicts the future in this case, but that the careful analyst discerns the preconditions for building a real future.

Thus a task is presented to the church for want of other organizations to handle it. It is not that the church is formally qualified to make up for the deficiencies of human society. It is not that revelation, or expertise in human affairs, or infused knowledge tells the church what procedures can and should be implemented. It is simply that the church is the object of a social demand stemming from the anxiety of various groups in the face of an uncertain, menacing future.

Even beyond the boundaries of its own religious audience in post-Christian societies, the church still continues to be delegated the authority to enlighten and help humanity in its quest for security and its avoidance of anxiety. It thus enjoys a potential store of ideological power that would entitle it to point out and stimulate the collective leap that industrialized societies must now make toward the required transformation of the world. To be sure, the church is often ill prepared and reticent, because its past misadventures in filling a supplementary role have been costly in terms of disengagement from outside influence. Pulled in the opposite direction by its own internal effort to return to its sources and get out of politics, it is inclined to resist appeals that do not clearly fall within its province.

But humanity needs a helping hand to cross the threshold where it now finds itself; it needs some injection of ethical values. The church has the mission to help human beings move beyond themselves, not only toward God but also toward the human tasks they must take in hand. Hence it is being challenged to shoulder the task of raising the consciousness of many persons who would pay no heed to it if it tried to lay down rules for forms of behavior that fall under their own competence and responsibility. They are willing to heed the church when it comes to seeking solutions for a disordered and increasingly uninhabitable world. They can find no other source of enlightenment, no other framework of action, in their efforts to transform the system that engenders underdevelopment. They are willing to place their confidence in the church insofar as it is ready to assume its "political" responsibilities on a worldwide scale.

A sense of guilt threatens to overtake the "privileged" when they discover the real effects of the system from which they are benefiting. It could intensify their resistance to needed change. On the other hand it is clearly one of the reasons why many who no longer frequent the church—because it helped to instill guilt feelings in them in the past—are willing to let the church step in and help them to convert their guilt into responsible initiatives.

The world is misshapen because its organization does not permit us to satisfy the needs of all human beings. The church has its share of responsibility for what produced this disorder, but it is in a position to make the disorder clear so that the process of reorganization may begin. And it seems to have more of a chance of being heard than do other organizations. When the sin of the world is laid bare in all its historical consequences, the church is qualified to help human beings and groups bear the weight of their responsibility and convert their acknowledgment into conscientization and mobilization.

The church seems to play a marginal role in societies that have emancipated themselves from its tutelage. Yet there are many indications that it is in a position to play new and unexpected roles in those societies, opening them up to their responsibilities in fashioning a new social order for the whole world. The church can help to stimulate the political will that is so desperately needed. As Pérez Guerrero, Third World co-president of the North-South Conference, has repeatedly pointed out, the absence of that political will in the industrialized countries has so far ruled out the possibility of negotiation.

The church has its own audience. It is still animated by the impulse that gave it birth; it has not been suffocated by its errors and faults. That impulse moves it toward the confession of sins and various processes of conversion. Thus the church finds itself in a paradoxical situation within the industrialized nations. They have felt obliged to exclude the church from their political debates. But when it comes to international policies, they need its help to ponder and implement those crucial issues on which the construction of a world society will depend.

To be sure, the church is not the only organization capable of playing a role in this policy shift. But it does have a responsibility here because only it can assume certain roles. It cannot escape this responsibility by appealing to the principle of a division of labor between clergy and laity, claiming that lay persons have all the more societal responsibility insofar as they have less responsibility in the church.

The church as an organized collectivity has a social role by virtue of its very existence. It is summoned to help move industrialized societies toward their new task, because they now constitute one of the main obstacles to systemic transformation. If the church were to absent itself from this critical turning point in history, claiming that it had been all too present in an earlier age, that decision would be fraught with dire consequences for both the church and humankind.

Thesis 17: The church has a role to play in resolving the contradictions of the world society taking shape.

The church is present an international life through all its varied institutions, ranging from the Holy See and the World Council of Churches to various Christian international organizations. The church plays a role in international life by the very fact that it exists and functions as in international organization.

It can and should contribute to the work of analysis that is one of the major requirements for the transformation of the global system. If the perversions of the system are not laid bare, the initiatives undertaken may be no more than palliative measures designed to keep its gears in operation. Only economic, sociological, and political analyses (to mention just a few) will bring to light the processes of destructuring and restructuring that are needed.

To be sure, the church is no better qualified or equipped than other organizations to handle this task. Moreover, even though it may have the human resources for such a task, it often delays in organizing them for the work at hand. In earlier times, by contrast, it did manage to organize associations to deal with human distress and protect the defenseless. The fact remains, however, that the church is in a position to mobilize resources and human personnel to research the new issues. It can help to make clear that international relationships must be reorganized, and it can point up the perspectives that flow from that realization.

The church does not have to defend the same interests espoused by public organizations of a national or international character. Its potential differs from that of many nongovernmental organizations as well. So it is in a position to create research locales and groups that, removed from the pull of immediate interests, might elaborate the strategies needed to reorganize the world system.

Espousing no specific policy itself and hence less liable to be suspected of trying to impose its own views, the church is in a position to provide investigative findings whose relevance would be more readily accepted. In such a context it might also have the courage and honesty to critically analyze its own role in past centuries. The fact is that the church has been more than a little involved in the creation of the world as it is now, with all its consequences of underdevelopment, injustice, and poverty.

That sort of critical analysis has been going on for some time, both within and without the church. Within the church it has occasioned resistance and trauma. It is now time for the church to pursue that analysis wholeheartedly, and to bring to public attention the dynamisms that have produced the present situation.

As the agency in charge of the civil religion of the West since the collapse of the Roman Empire, the church has been one of the chief protagonists in the colonial adventure. Every human enterprise needs legitimation, and it was the church that legitimated the colonial enterprise. It entrusted the conquerors with the task of evangelizing the peoples they went out to exploit or exterminate. Hence it bears ideological responsibility for that history. It may well have found itself in competition with, or opposition to, the bourgeois classes that gradually came to power and sought to emancipate themselves from the church. But even as Western societies emancipated themselves from the church, it remained in alliance with the rising middle classes. Church representatives may have tried to defend colonized peoples. But that does not alter the fact that the gospel message was perverted insofar as it was used to induce resignation in those peoples. We must now reexamine that history closely and scrupulously in order to fully comprehend the world it has produced.

To the extent that the church takes this work upon itself, it will be qualified to point up what is untenable and intolerable in international life today. Its own audience will help the vast majority of the world population to envision a new reading of reality and to take apart the certitudes inculcated by the dominant ideology. The Holy See and the World Council of Churches have already taken on that task. The addresses of Pope Paul VI to international organizations helped to frame the basis for a critical analysis of relationships between the underdeveloped countries and the industrialized nations.

This work of critical analysis is increasingly bound to become the priority task of Third World intellectuals: economists, sociologists, historians, and others. The church will be involved with them. Indeed it is already involved by virtue of its Third World theologians, who are working in fellowship with the defeated and oppressed of history. Their work of clarification is enabling their peoples to understand the causes of their dependence and to take upon themselves the process of liberation.

This critical and constructive effort in theology is shifting the focus of the church from the center to the periphery. Its perspectives are changed as it seeks to comprehend the good news proclaimed to the poor and to live the faith in the process of transforming the world.

On a planetary scale the church constitutes a definite socio-cultural locale.

New ideas have a better chance of being heard and implemented there than in many other international frameworks. There will of course be resistance to "subversive" readings of history and of de facto reality. But disconcerting as their aims and claims may be, the poor always end up making themselves heard and understood in the church. The ecclesial conscience, like any collective conscience, tends to cringe before ideas that shake its constellation of certitudes. Yet sensitivity to the cry of the poor persists, because it is part and parcel of the divine message that gives being and shape to the church.

Quite aside from noble sentiments, which are not to be scorned, the Christian ethos is basically predisposed to pay heed to the poor, to those who are the victims of a society badly organized. It may well be that for long periods of time the Christian ethos had little or no effect on collective conduct, but that does not rule out the possibility of its becoming effective in unexpected ways. There are many indications that something of the sort is happening right now among various church groups.

We are witnessing a sharp demographic shift in the church, away from the old centers of Christendom and toward the once colonized peripheries. There is good reason to expect a sharp turn in the collective awareness of the ecclesial universe. The majority of Christians are to be found in the Third World, and their "young churches" are presently engaged in the task of working out their own theologies and ecclesial organizations. More and more it will be their voices that will be heard in the universal church, and hence in the world. Their practice of the faith revolves around situations that are matters of life and death. Hence their message will be all the more significant insofar as it stems from the rediscovery of the word of God within a historical movement akin to that which led to the elaboration of sacred history in the first place. As the church of the poor takes the floor, we shall find that its message to the world has much to do with the issues involved in world reorganization.

What the church has had to say to the world has not been without relevance to international life in the past, particularly in the recent decades. It has reflected the practices of those Christians most deeply involved in analyzing and transforming the structures that have produced underdevelopment. Paul VI's *Populorum Progressio* was particularly noteworthy. Calling development the new name for peace, he vigorously pointed up the necessity of transforming any system that blocked development. Insofar as the universal church speaks out on the basis of church awareness and experience in the Third World, its message will be more pointed and pertinent. It will then contribute far more to the formation and mobilization of world public opinion.

There is reason to hope that the church will heed and understand what is said about the world scene within its own parameters. More than once in the past the church has managed to mobilize itself for far more doubtful causes. If it can now mobilize itself in a crusade against underdevelopment, injustice, and poverty, it would be an incomparable force for the audacious transformations that are needed.

Generous-minded proposals and publicly endorsed values rarely constitute the heart of political policies. But there are moments in history when an added impetus, an injection of ethical, spiritual, theological motivation, is needed to move societies above and beyond themselves toward the future that must be built. The issue at hand for us has to do with crossing the threshold to a new history, one that will truly be a history of humanity on a planetary scale, one in which humanity will truly be in communication with itself and actively involved in collective creativity. At such a time every source of inspiration and energy is called upon to face the challenge and do its part, and the church is no exception.

The church may be fearful of helping to rivet the attention of men and women on their earthly tasks, of losing its ability to lead them to God. However, its own deepest tradition summons it to run that risk. Otherwise it may fail to uphold the glory of God that is to be found in every human being living from the life of God. Fear of losing God's trail, or of compromising with those who erase it from their own lives, should not deter the church from the task that it faces. Where the church is most alive today, and that may include its monasteries and islands of silent solitude, it has already come to grips with history in the making and it is already paving the way for the "revolution in solidarity" that must take place before the end of this millennium.

The international role of the church will depend on its efforts at conscientization in both underdeveloped and developed nations. From those efforts it will accumulate experience in its collective memory and consciousness. Thus it will have its own specific contribution to make to ongoing debates and negotiations on which the establishment of a new international economic order will depend. Insofar as the church has ties of solidarity with the peoples of the Third World, who are the source of this international undertaking, it is in a position to serve as a mediator between their rightful aspirations and the well-taken interests of the industrialized nations.

Having learned from its past mistakes and from criticism of them, the church is unlikely to succumb to the allurements of power associated with its ideological or political roles. Having only recently extricated itself from the perils of triumphalism, the church is now able to join the collective task in a spirit of humility and service. That task needs all the forces of good will and organized effort it can find. The worst thing for the church and humankind would be for the church to absent itself from the present moment in history, which is truly a *kairos*, a moment of grace.

Thesis 18: The roles proposed for the church, or required of it, derive from its mission to proclaim the gospel to the poor.

Over the past twenty years or so, much effort has gone into analyzing underdevelopment and exploring ways to spur development. It has become increasingly clear that development cannot be reduced to economic growth, however much it is part of development. Development is primarily a political, cultural, and even spiritual problem.

Constructing a new international economic order is, in fact, *the* object of international politics. For politics is nothing else than the ongoing negotiation of contradictions between social groups and the construction of relationship systems enabling or coercing them to intermesh with one another.

For such social transformations to be possible, however, it is necessary to unlock and dismantle the mental structures that induce one group to resignation and the other group to self-satisfied possession of a well-being for which the first group must pay the price. Societies clearly need a new ethical and spiritual impetus to change their old ways of thinking and acting.

The church is certainly hesitant about undertaking the political task to which it is being summoned. At great expense it learned that societies are the active subjects of their own revolutions. But it is more inclined to play a role in the conscientization of various human groups and the elucidation of the tasks to be undertaken.

In the reality of history, however, these different tasks cannot be dissociated. Mental and social structures are so interrelated that it is impossible to deal adequately with one set of structures if the other is neglected. Political activity cannot disregard its cultural and spiritual effects. Spiritual or cultural conscientization cannot disregard its political effects. Hence those who decide to work for development are led to involve themselves in the elaboration and implementation of an international political strategy. To conceal these interrelated involvements would be to shirk full disclosure of the reality we face, the reality on which we must act if life on a habitable earth is to be possible.

The church has suffered a great deal in trying to liberate itself from its past involvements in world affairs. It is understandably hesitant when it is faced with new involvements in politics. In seeking to find its identity once again as the body of Jesus Christ, the church shrank from the prospect of new political involvements. It went back to the word of God so that it would have a better chance of pointing out the perspectives that open up to human beings both in and beyond their basic production tasks. This clarification and differentiation of roles in post-Christian societies was necessary and painful, and we cannot turn a blind eye to its lessons. The church has the mission of helping human beings to live in relationship with God and hence in communion with one another. It cannot depart from that role and try once again to take the place of organizations that societies must construct for their own needs.

On the other hand the church exists in given societies, and in the global society now taking shape. Hence it is implicated in societal dynamics and cannot abstract itself from them. In its own practices, therefore, the church must see to it that its direct or indirect interventions in politics stimulate societies without stripping them of their ability to control their own dynamics. If this is to be done, there must be ongoing negotiation between the structuring of human groups as churches and their structuring as societies.

Relatively autonomous in structuring itself, the church must be able to do this in line with the main thrust of the historical movement from which it springs. Its collective memory of that movement is singularly determining. To exist as the church of Jesus Christ, the church must so perform and delineate its practices that those assembled within it can see them as an implementation of the faith that they hold. This work of the church on itself, of regulating and interpreting its own activity in history, is as important for the church as is its participation in history-in-the-making. Indeed it is important for all those who rely on the church, whether they be members of the church or simply have contact with its institutions and representative organizations.

This coherence, which must be worked at continually, is a requirement for the church's identification. It is also a criterion of the correctness of the church's presence in the world. Consistency between the intrinsic dynamism of the church and its linkages with societal dynamics is never rigidly fixed in some stifling orthodoxy. But it has more importance for the church than for any other organized collectivity because the existence of the church is predicated on the assembly of those who adhere to the message entrusted to it.

It is important, then, that the roles envisioned for the church in fashioning a new world dovetail with its mission—that is, to preach the gospel message and enable those who heed it to live their lives accordingly.

Helping human groups to take charge of their destiny, to gain a better handle on their relationship to the sacred, or to God, comes down to proclaiming the word of God, who invites every human being to fashion a life in the divine image and likeness by building the world and liberating humanity from every obstacle to human growth. The good news proclaimed to the poor does not invite them to resignation but to hope and a sense of responsibility.

The participation of the church in the conscientization of groups in enforced dependence flows from the obvious thrust of its evangelizing mission. It is both a precondition for and a requirement of that mission. The gospel message cannot be received or interiorized without setting in motion an underground process: the cultural reactivation of the groups who adhere to it. In-depth evangelization calls for the reinterpretation of indigenous religious traditions in the light of the gospel, and for comprehension of the gospel in the light of indigenous traditions. That two-way process is one of the factors involved in development.

Neither one being subordinated to the other, the tasks of evangelization and conscientization are so closely bound up that they cannot be dissociated, though it may be useful to distinguish them for purposes of analysis. All the basic processes of church life—preaching, catechesis, pastoral care, and so forth—can and should contribute to conscientization. To the extent that they do, they cannot help but further the desired effect of evangelization: that persons lead their lives in the kind of relationship with God that they seek to inculcate. In de facto experience this convergence or identification of evangelization and development is so clear and obvious that it is useless to prolong the either/or debate that assumes we must choose between the two. A conscientizing evangelization can disturb only those who dread the subversive—creative—power of the gospel message.

Much of the same holds true for the formation of public opinion in the industrialized nations. Insofar as the church participates in this process, it is led to point up the injustice stemming from unsound international relationships, the contradiction between a badly organized world and the plan of God. It thus invites its members to get involved in the transformation of the world in order to undergo conversion to the gospel and to live in accord with their conversion. Here again evangelization and conscientization converge in response to the same imperative. The transformation of the world becomes one of the criteria for the authenticity of our faith. As the 1971 Synod of Bishops puts it in *Justice in the World*: "Action on behalf of justice and participation in the transformation of the world fully appear to us as a constitutive dimension of the preaching of the gospel . . . of the church's mission for the redemption of the human race and its liberation from every oppressive situation" (n. 6).

The church was made aware of development problems by the discovery of famine and hunger in the world. At first it appealed to the demands of charity to mobilize its members for a campaign against world hunger and in favor of aid to the Third World. Some twenty years later, it began to realize that it must participate in the transformations needed in the world system; that such participation tests the truth of its faith and the relevance or meaningfulness of the gospel that it proclaims. The 1971 text marks the pivotal point in that change of perspective, a change that is still producing its shock waves.

This also helps clarify the role that the church should play in highlighting and effecting necessary transformations in the world system. The church is an international organization and hence participates in international life. It can help to promote analyses that will dismantle old certitudes and commonplaces about world organization, and it can help to further negotiations designed to ensure new international relationships. This new role is indeed a more political one for the church, but it is entirely consistent with the proclamation of the gospel. In the case of the Roman Catholic Church, of course, that role should not be delegated solely to the Holy See by an indifferent Catholic clergy and laity.

The gospel message passes judgment on the world—not to condemn it but to save it. It brings to light what is hidden, what can continue to function only insofar as it remains invisible. The gospel summons us to analyze reality, even as Jesus did. When Jesus commented on the tie between Caesar and his coinage, he made clear the vanity of Caesar's pretensions to divinity: a tax collector no longer had any right to make demands in the name of divine worship.

As doctrine and praxis, the gospel message fosters societal analysis. The church certainly is not betraying the gospel when it participates in societal analysis and the negotiation of societal transformations. Indeed it is doing its part to let the gospel sound out more clearly, to let it be understood more profoundly. In many instances it is no longer a question of the church's resorting to the gospel to find out what it means for the church. Instead it is up to the church to help create attitudes, behavior patterns, and societal situations that will render its message intelligible and meaningful.

A great misunderstanding is paralyzing the church, holding it back from more active involvement in the struggle for development. It is the notion that the problem at issue is a "temporal" problem. The claim is made that it is not the church's business, although humanity is confronted with a matter of life or death. When it chooses for life, the church has to pay the price of that commitment.

Chapter 5

Traditional Practices Coincident with Roles the Church Must Now Assume

If the church is to be capable of assuming the roles now proposed to it, it must explore once again its collective memory, its history, and its prehistory. There it will find key moments characterized by active resistance to the structuring of societies in inequality and to the sacralization of their injustice. The legislative efforts of ancient Israel, the preaching of the prophets, the praxis of Jesus, and the theological work of the church fathers illustrate a central dynamic in a normative tradition. That tradition must become better known if we are to rediscover the gospel as a divine force for the transformation of the world.

Thesis 19: The gospel—the good news proclaimed to the poor—is a divine force for the transformation of the world.

The worst fate to befall the gospel message, in terms of the inner dynamics of its history, would be to have it seen as a message from another world that leaves this world as it stands. So viewed, the gospel message would dissociate its earnest followers from the collective effort of humankind to make the earth habitable for all.

The gospel is the word of God, of course. As such, its first and last aim is to bring out our relationship to God as the most important structure of human existence. This evident certitude is so basic a part of the gospel universe that it automatically serves as the chief reference point in elucidating the radical nature of our relationship to others: love of neighbor is identified with love of God. To ground our whole life on this relationship to God is not, however, to live out the history of some other world. It is to unveil the first and last structure of this world, where human beings fashion themselves into humanity as best they can.

To be sure, the gospel does recount a passage from a starting point *here* to a culminating fulfillment *there*, beyond anything we might imagine or conceive. Abraham and Moses serve as two images of that process. The point of fulfil-

59

ment is always described in terms of images: promised land, eternal city, wedding banquet, and so forth. But it must be remembered that the distant point of fulfilment functions as do symbols. In short, it gives reality and existence to the *journey*, imbuing it with movement and impetus. It undergirds life as an active quest for fulfilment, as a search for communion in the sovereign liberty of God's offspring.

The gospel message is the word of God that sets human beings on their journey toward fulfilled existence in God. It is not the daydream of a humanity incapable of mastering its destiny, a humanity doomed to impotence by "the gods." The gospel message is a force at work within this world, depositing the seed that will enable it to achieve life in all its fulness.

The gospel is not a discourse on reality calculated to make reality tolerable because it cannot be changed. The gospel is unlike any exposition that tells us what is behind what we see, or any exposition that tells us what ought to be. The gospel is the word that does what it says because it speaks of life in terms of its desire and demand for communion. In the depths of history-in-the-making, the gospel message creates the world by transforming it so that it may be organized in terms of true human progress and what it requires.

It is obvious that the gospel is not a political treatise; nor does it recount a political praxis. In an even more radical way, nevertheless, it is a message that subverts all the organizations created by human beings to guide their societal life; for those organizations inevitably subject the poor to the rich, the weak to the strong. Enjoying the power of God, who speaks through it, the gospel message puts down the mighty from their thrones, exalts those of low degree, fills the hungry with good things, and sends the rich away empty (Luke 1:52–53). It is the supremely subversive word, speaking the truth and thereby revealing human constructs for what they are. They govern the collective life of human beings only by conveying the illusion that they are normal and perennial.

It is not surprising, indeed it is reassuring, to know that the power of the gospel has not really functioned in history for very long periods of time. The gospel poses a danger to human dreams insofar as human beings organize societies only by fabricating deities and imposing them as natural and inevitable when, in fact, those deities are their own imaginary creation. When God reveals himself as God, those deities crumble and the certitudes sacralized by them disappear into thin air. God alone is God. In God's presence nothing remains sacred except human beings, perhaps, insofar as they consecrate themselves to God in service to their fellow humans.

This is the theoretical principle, practiced at certain rare points in the history of Christianity, that can regulate and control the irrepressible human tendency to submit to counterfeit deities. Those who recognize and acknowledge God as God can no longer bow to other deities. Enjoying the sovereign liberty of God's children, they are no longer enslaved to any law, even though it may be presented as a divine law. They know that even the Sabbath—the time in life set aside for the worship of God—is made for the human being, not the human being for the Sabbath. They know that Caesar may be entitled to collect the taxes needed for the conduct of societal life; but they know too that he can make no claims to divinity. They will pay him his money but refuse him worship, even at the risk of undermining societal certitudes and organizations. That is what the very first Christians did vis-à-vis the Roman Empire. Respecting its laws, they undermined its whole setup.

The gospel message wells up from a millennial history of militant believers who accepted the fact that God alone is God. Knowing that, they repeatedly tried to oppose idolatry and its effects. They challenged the human tendency to self-exaltation, or to further self-abasement before the inertial tendency of society toward inequality.

Residing above the stars that served as calendric measurements and below the watery depths entrusted to human mastery, God imposed his reality upon the Jewish people. Surrounded by gods, they were a people without a god. So they labored to organize themselves into the people of God, seeking to direct their communal life without submitting to any idol. Pledged to the worship of God, they organized as a people to resist the temptation to fashion gods; but time and again, as we know, they succumbed to that very temptation.

Their resistance to idolatry went hand in hand with resistance to inequality. Marked by repeated failures and fresh starts, their history is of singular signifi- cance because it left traces not only in the memory of the community but also in written texts. The structure of other traditional societies, less well known to us, may well bear similar witness to such resistance; but it is usually impossible to figure out the regulative procedures and processes whereby those societies managed to put up a defense against inertial tendencies. It is different in the case of the millennial practices underlying the gospel message and its resist- ance to the societal sacralization of inequality. They can be reconstructed on the basis of written texts whose socio-political import and thrust are ascertain- able.

By virtue of its shockingly radical nature, the gospel led to a utopia—the one in practice in the first communist community of Jerusalem. Nostalgia for that community, projected into the future, imbues every variety of messianism: Marxist messianism, to begin with, which is the most typical of them all. In like manner, nostalgia for the egalitarianism of nomadic society was projected into the messianism of ancient Israel. But in the gospel message there is some- thing buried even more deeply than is utopian communion. In its proclama- tion of blessedness for the poor we find the memory of a praxis designed to organize society in such a way that there will no longer be any poor persons in it.

That praxis, always doomed to failure, has come down to us through the ages, along with the message that makes explicit its thrust and import. Both open up new perspectives for us. The message may be less exalting than are visions of utopia; but if it is taken seriously, it can also be more operative and effective in helping us to master societal dynamics.

The gospel is neither political nor social, but centered around a God who continually re-creates the world by summoning human beings to transform it so that they may live in the divine image and likeness. Then the gospel will show up in all its theological radicality as a divine force for the ever continuing transfor- mation of provisional organizations on which human existence and fulfilment depend. The gospel message establishes a criterion for the worship of God: love for one's fellow human beings and service to them, starting with the poor

and defenseless. In so doing, it establishes the right of the poor to claim their
share of the resources necessary for human existence and to participate in the
organization of the relevant production processes. By setting human beings
on the road to God, the gospel message gives them the earth to shape and
manage.

Moving beyond all the apparent contradictions between worship of God and
human creative work, the gospel message is a rousing summons to establish a
social order in which no one will be neglected. It is utopian in the sense that it
proclaims a never-ending set of tasks to which persons dedicate themselves
because those tasks must be carried out; they do not ask themselves whether
those tasks are impossible or not. It is not exactly the same thing as mobilizing
groups to realize dreams.

One of those impossible but necessary tasks is shaping societal and international life to meet the needs of all. Every source of inspiration and every available force must be mobilized to achieve it. The gospel message is one of the
prime resources available to us, but many believers no longer realize it because
they have lost the memory of its thrust and import. We must once again
explore the collective memory embodied in, and symbolized by, the gospel
message.

**Thesis 20: From beginning to end the Judeo-Christian tradition is marked by a
series of discontinuous efforts to regulate the tendency of societies to
be structured in terms of inequality.**

Societies take shape in history by continually organizing and reorganizing the
structures that will enable them to articulate and implement their operative
relationships. Collective awareness tends to be polarized around organizations
needed to make up for the defects of those already in place. But it is worth
pointing out, however banal the observation may be, that the underlying structures of social dynamics often go back a long way. Deeply buried in the collective consciousness, they have come to be taken for granted as "natural" or
"eternal." We can hardly imagine that they were originally created to meet
certain needs of the day.

Those who must cross linguistic boundaries to communicate with others have
come to realize what a patchwork quilt is imposed on us by linguistic structures.
One language can say something easily, it seems, but there is no ready counter-
part in some other language. Speech and interlinguistic communication seem
almost impossible. In learning to speak a certain language, every human being is
routed on the track of an age-old linguistic experience that will profoundly
affect his or her representations and patterns of behavior. And the influence will
be all the more effective insofar as it becomes unconscious.

Consider the various efforts by human groups to organize time, to do the
impossible task of combining the solar year, the lunar month, and the ordinary
day. And then there are the seasons and other regular cycles of nature. All these
efforts create differences in collective representations and living patterns. Those
differences seem unimportant until one particular system overlaps with another.
To get some feeling for the possible complexity of the ordinary week, for exam-

ple, consider a country where Jews, Christians, and Muslims live together without any one group dominating the others. How complicated it is to blend lifestyles centered around different days of the week—in this case Friday, Saturday, and Sunday!

The organization of space reveals the same sort of complexity insofar as it serves different interests: hunting, food gathering, agriculture, herding, urban or rural residence, and the like. It bears witness to the millennial efforts of human beings to agree on arrangements for their coexistence on earth. The rules governing access to water, arable land, and exchange points were often established in the remote past.

Thanks to the work of ethnologists, historians, sociologists, and others, we now have better insight into the rules governing kinship and trade relationships in a wide variety of societies. It is evident that basic patterns of conduct often derive from norms that were originally established to deal with needs very different from the ones faced today. Organizations established to promote cultivation of the soil may not be the most useful when it comes to mining the subsoil.

Such examples could be cited indefinitely, and they may have something to offer us as we seek to negotiate current contradictions between societies. They suggest that we would do well to explore the collective human memory, its past history, and the traces it has left on the various strata superimposed on the human unconscious or the surface of the planet.

The Judeo-Christian tradition is one such heritage. Closer study of that tradition might offer us new perspectives in approaching the formidable problems associated with redistributing resources, production activities, and revenues among the various groups that make up the human species. I am not suggesting that we can find our own model there. The Chinese are right in saying that models are not transferable. But in that tradition we can find traces of original attempts to regulate the dynamics of society.

The ancient Hebrews were nomads who settled down to a sedentary way of life. Or they grew out of a confederation of nomadic tribes living on the borderlands between desert and arable land. They were brought together as a people by the worship of Yahweh, who was recognized as the creator of the stars above and the depths below, as well as the liberator of the enslaved and oppressed. Acknowledging God's sovereignty over all things, the Hebrews were imbued with a keen sense of solidarity and equality. Inasmuch as everything came from God, it was unthinkable that the lowliest of God's people should be abandoned to harsh fate if they failed to succeed in life.

Ancient Israel was certainly not a people of saints and sages. Many parts of the Bible are far from being an edifying history. Societal perversion in all its forms and effects can be found there. The strong were superior to the weak; the rich grew richer and the poor struggled for mere survival. As the nomadic herdsmen became farmers, artisans, and merchants, and as complex relationships developed between town and countryside, inequality of opportunity and position spread in Israel as in every society.

What is worth remembering about that particular societal experience is the fact that efforts were made to regulate and control the distortions. We still have traces of those efforts, even though they did not meet with success. We find significant indications of a long-term collective effort to break with the inertial tendency of society toward structural inequality.

Such was the role of the sabbatical year, whose rules can be found in various legislative codes (Exod. 23:10–13; Deut. 15:1–8; Lev. 25:2–7). Vestiges of those rules can also be found in the historical writings. The sabbatical year was the last year of each "week" of years. In that year the land was to lie fallow. Its fruits were to be left to the poor, slaves were to be freed, and debtors were to be released from their debts. We can find allusions to the countless problems raised by such a law, but it is difficult to verify the extent to which it was actually implemented. Nevertheless it is worth noting that such a law was drafted in fairly ancient times, and that no equivalent is evident among neighboring peoples.

The seventh day was a day of rest set aside for the worship of Yahweh. It served as the model for the sabbatical division of time over longer periods, underlining the importance of fidelity to the covenant. The significant thing about the sabbath-year law is the connection established between surrender to God and the arbitrary or relative character of social structures based on luck, competence, or an enterprising spirit. Productive individuals were to leave things up to God in the seventh year, relying on the results of the six preceding years and almost certainly devising ways to preserve surpluses. Those who had been unproductive, whether or not due to their own fault, were assured of being able to try their luck again at the legally appointed time. This practice of a moratorium helped to stall the tendency of social organizations to become fixed, rigid, and sacred. Nothing was ever acquired once and for all, for better or for worse.

The jubilee year (Lev. 25: 8–17, 23–55) came at the end of seven weeks of years—that is, the fiftieth year. It went even further in disestablishing the social system. Besides the stipulations of the sabbatical year, it also called for the recovery of fields and houses that had been alienated for whatever reason. It thus underlined the provisional nature of land transactions and others on which the subsistence and freedom of the poor and the helpless depended. Because everything belonged to God, the means of production and basic consumer goods could not be monopolized by only a few. Because the entire people had been freed from bondage in Egypt by God, no one could be reduced to slavery once and for all. Here, even more clearly than in the sabbatical-year law, recognition of God as God worked against the sacralization of social structures based on the law of the strongest.

Such a jubilee law would be bound to produce social upheavals. The absence of any traces of such upheavals suggests that this highly utopian standard was never really implemented. Perhaps the technological, economic, and social preconditions for its application were missing. We find similar ideals in the New Testament—for example, the elimination of distinctions between free human beings and slaves, and an invitation to treat slaves as fellow human beings (Gal. 3:28; Philem. 8–21). Their social implementation had to await centuries of development and transformation, both in the means of production and production relationships.

In like manner, at one time there was no slavery in the grain regions of Gaul, where a rudimentary reaper had been invented. But it was later introduced there, as elsewhere in the Mediterranean world, because it was part and parcel of the social structure of the Roman Empire. It became unthinkable only after the invention of the rigid horse collar and the exploitation of other energy sources.

Even though efforts were initiated in ancient Israel to stem the tide of social inequality, they may not have really worked in practice because the proper conditions for their implementation were not at hand. Such time-lags between collective awareness of the need to control social dynamics and the actual ability to do so should not astonish those who now see the need to create a new international economic order.

The important point here is that a voluntarist effort to control social inequities was attempted by the Hebrews as they moved from a pastoral way of life to a commercial economy. Nostalgia for the egalitarianism of nomadic life was undoubtedly involved. But even more decisive and important was religion itself and its picture of the relationship between God and humanity. Hebrew religion saw God as the liberator, the lord of history, and the master of the world and its peoples. It is well to emphasize this religious effort to desacralize inequitable social organizations: the commonplace view is that religion has the function of legitimating them.

To repeat, I am not suggesting that we should look to the efforts of the ancient Hebrews for our model. The very fact that their model may never actually have been put into operation would be enough to discourage such transfers. What is worth noting here is the spirit or awareness underlying that model. Although it may seem original in its own context, the fact is that we find similar procedures and efforts in many traditional societies to put up real resistance to inequitable social structuring.

Contrary to the view taken for granted in populous, centralized societies, inequality is not automatically accepted. The instinctive reactions against injustice by its victims are not as sentimental and utopian as many are led to believe. Egalitarianism does remain a dream, to be sure. But active resistance to the inevitability of inequality can become a social practice that eventually devises the norms and mechanisms required for its functioning.

Even defeats and failures can shed light on the subject. They point us in the right direction by highlighting the obstacles that human beings must overcome in order to fashion themselves into a human species. Victory over seemingly insurmountable obstacles is possible. It is in that perspective that we do well to ponder the seemingly ridiculous and futile efforts of ancient Israel. Certainly those who hearken back to that tradition should not be too quick to underestimate the structural relationship between recognition of God as God and the course of social dynamics. God may not point out the right road to us. But God does indicate that certain approaches are doomed to failure.

Thesis 21: The struggle for justice—the struggle against injustice—is one of the main features of the praxis and preaching of the prophets, who were charged with watching over the people's fidelity to God.

The many texts of the Hebrew prophets must be read against the backdrop of Israel's legislative efforts to resist inequality. Those prophetic texts insist on the radical incompatibility between worship of God and exploitation of the poor.

Because the law proved inadequate in regulating social relationships, men of God rose up time and again to proclaim that those who were expropriating lands, goods, and power were being unfaithful to the covenant.

In ancient Israel, it is true, wealth was considered a divine blessing whereas poverty was considered a punishment for laziness or a disordered life. But deep concern for the proper balance between poverty and wealth bears witness to a keen sense of the cause-effect relationship between the two. We find this striking evocation in the Book of Job:

> Men remove landmarks; they seize flocks and pasture them. They drive away the ass of the fatherless; they take the widow's ox for a pledge. They thrust the poor off the road; the poor of the earth all hide themselves. Behold, like wild asses in the desert they go forth to their toil, seeking prey in the wilderness as food for their children. They gather their fodder in the field as they glean the vineyard of the wicked man. They lie all night naked, without clothing, and have no covering in the cold. They are wet with the rain of the mountains, and cling to the rock for want of shelter. (There are those who snatch the fatherless child from the breast, and take in pledge the infant of the poor.) They go about naked, without clothing; hungry, they carry the sheaves; among the olive rows of the wicked they make oil; they tread the wine presses, but suffer thirst. From out of the city the dying groan, and the soul of the wounded cries for help; yet God pays no attention to their prayer [24:2-12].

As injustice becomes more pervasive, God seems to remain silent. The vituperative denunciations of the prophets are a response to this seeming scandal. In God's name the prophets speak out against the practices of the powerful and the rich, who oppress the weak and the poor. Laying bare those practices, the prophets call down God's curse on the perpetrators:

> Hear this, you who trample upon the needy, and bring the poor of the land to an end, saying, "When will the new moon be over, that we may sell grain? And the sabbath, that we may offer wheat for sale, that we may make the ephah small and the shekel great, and deal deceitfully with false balances, that we may buy the poor for silver and the needy for a pair of sandals, and sell the refuse of the wheat?" The Lord has sworn by the pride of Jacob: "Surely I will never forget any of their deeds. Shall not the land tremble on this account, and every one mourn who dwells in it, and all of it rise like the Nile, and be tossed about and sink again, like the Nile of Egypt?" [Amos 8:4-8].

It is not by chance that the exploitation of the poor is linked with idolatry, the supreme form of infidelity to God. One example:

> Thus says the Lord: ". . . Because they sell the righteous for silver, and the needy for a pair of shoes—they that trample the head of the poor into the

dust of the earth, and turn aside the way of the afflicted; a man and his father go in to the same maiden, so that my holy name is profaned; they lay themselves down beside every altar upon garments taken in pledge; and in the house of their God they drink the wine of those who have been fined. . . . You made the Nazirites drink wine, and commanded the prophets, saying, 'You shall not prophesy.' Behold, I will press you down in your place, as a cart full of sheaves presses down. Flight shall perish from the swift, and the strong shall not retain his strength, nor shall the mighty save his life; he who handles the bow shall not stand, and he who is swift of foot shall not save himself, nor shall he who rides the horse save his life; and he who is stout of heart among the mighty shall flee away naked in that day," says the Lord [Amos 2:6–16].

Protesting against the established disorder, the prophets announce the coming of God to turn the whole situation upside down:

The meek shall obtain fresh joy in the Lord, and the poor among men shall exult in the Holy One of Israel. For the ruthless shall come to nought and the scoffer cease, and all who watch to do evil shall be cut off, who by a word make a man out to be an offender, and lay a snare for him who reproves in the gate, and with an empty plea turn aside him who is in the right [Isa. 29:19–21].

The prophets summon the people to conversion, to put back into effect the social conventions that are part and parcel of the covenant. They point up the ethical and social import of fasting, for example, which is a typical step in the process of conversion to God:

Cry aloud, spare not, lift up your voice like a trumpet; declare to my people their transgression, to the house of Jacob their sins. Yet they seek me daily, and delight to know my ways, as if they were a nation that did righteousness and did not forsake the ordinance of their God; they ask of me righteous judgments, they delight to draw near to God. "Why have we fasted, and thou seest it not? Why have we humbled ourselves, and thou takest no knowledge of it?" Behold, in the day of your fast you seek your own pleasure, and oppress all your workers. Behold, you fast only to quarrel and to fight, and to hit with wicked fist. Fasting like yours this day will not make your voice to be heard on high. . . . Is not this the fast that I choose: to loose the bonds of wickedness, to undo the thongs of the yoke, to let the oppressed go free, and to break every yoke? Is it not to share your bread with the hungry, and bring the homeless poor into your house; when you see the naked, to cover him, and not to hide yourself from your own flesh? Then shall your light break forth like the dawn, and your healing shall spring up speedily; your righteousness shall go before you, the glory of the Lord shall be your rear guard. Then you shall call, and the Lord will answer; you shall cry, and he will say, Here I am [Isa. 58:1–9].

It is not just fasting that finds its verification in the practice of justice and righteousness as embodied in the law. Even sacrifices are meaningless unless social relationships are equitable:

> I hate, I despise your feasts, and I take no delight in your solemn assemblies. Even though you offer me your burnt offerings and cereal offerings, I will not accept them, and the peace offerings of your fatted beasts I will not look upon. Take away from me the noise of your songs; to the melody of your harps I will not listen. But let justice roll down like waters, and righteousness like an ever-flowing stream. Did you bring to me sacrifices and offerings the forty years in the wilderness, O house of Israel? [Amos 5:21-25].

The solidarity of the desert is evoked as the ideal of the society that is to be built in fidelity to the covenant. However real or imagined the former may be, we find the same language expressed in the Book of Isaiah:

> What to me is the multitude of your sacrifices? says the Lord. I have had enough of burnt offerings of rams and the fat of fed beasts. I do not delight in the blood of bulls, or of lambs, or of he-goats. When you come to appear before me, who requires of you this trampling of my courts? Bring no more vain offerings; incense is an abomination to me. New moon and sabbath and the calling of assemblies—I cannot endure iniquity and solemn assembly. Your new moons and your appointed feasts my soul hates; they have become a burden to me, I am weary of bearing them. When you spread forth your hands, I will hide my eyes from you; even though you make many prayers, I will not listen; your hands are full of blood. Wash yourselves; make yourselves clean; remove the evil of your doings from before my eyes; cease to do evil, learn to do good; seek justice, correct oppression; defend the fatherless, plead for the widow [Isa. 1:11-17].

In these texts we see surfacing the conflicts between the prophets and the priestly caste. The prophets are men of God, concerned about the plight of the poor. The priests are cultic officials; their ties are with the king and his authority. A social conflict shines through the prophet's challenge to cultic worship in the name of justice. God is called to witness and arbitrate the conflict, in terms of a court case. But Yahweh is the God of the covenant, around which Israelite society was structured in the first place. The prophetic texts can be appreciated only if we see them in connection with the legislative texts wherein the Israelites sought to keep track of their fidelity to the solidarity and egalitarianism of nomadic life. They inscribe the demand for justice and equality on the religious conscience of Israel, and then they link all that to authentic worship of God.

The conflict between priests and prophets arises from the fact that religious consciousness is always in danger of setting itself up institutionally as a social authority, an organized power centered around cultic worship. To offset this tendency one must appeal to God in order to challenge the social order or disorder that is thus sacralized. This dialectical tension points up both the "impossibility" and the necessity of controlling the inevitable processes of sacralization, of desacralizing societal institutions when it must be done. Both sacralization and desacralization, then, are intrinsic elements in societal dynamics.

Risking their tranquility and their lives, the Hebrew prophets spoke out forcefully. They could do so because the conscience, or bad conscience, of the people and its rulers was attuned to their message. The Israelites knew that their societal structure was bound up with their fidelity to Yahweh. That fidelity accounted for their existence as a people. The federated Hebrew tribes were held together only by their relationship to Yahweh, who was the ground of their language and of their societal structures. Behind the revolutionary texts of the prophets we can see the ongoing effort of a society to organize itself in such a way that it will remain faithful to the demands of solidarity.

The relativization of cultic worship is nonetheless striking when we consider that the Israelites existed as a people only insofar as they continued to choose to be Yahweh's people. They were God's people—and recognized as such by God—only to the extent that their organized life continued to ensure an equitable division of goods by imposing necessary constraints.

As I noted earlier, there is no question of simply transposing the comments of the Hebrew prophets on Israelite society to cover the contradictions evident in our nascent world society. But those who see the Judeo-Christian tradition as their own cannot remain insensitive to the biblical debate, which centered around the issue of organizing worship of God in such a way that it would be done "in spirit and in truth." The biblical texts have something important to say to the church as it mobilizes to assume its responsibility for the transformation of the world.

Thesis 22: The praxis and preaching of Jesus highlight the right of the poor to participate in community life and its fruits.

It is relatively easy to point out the socio-political import of divine worship in the Old Testament. But we encounter almost insurmountable resistance when it comes to a similar analysis of the words and deeds of Jesus of Nazareth. Provocative depictions of him as a revolutionary or a guerrilla fighter have only hardened that resistance, which stems from a long tradition of "spiritualizing" him. As a result, his followers have long found it difficult to view him as a human being. The age-old work of the church on its representations of Christ (divine and human being) must be taken up again and again. It must follow the same course as the church's work on its representations of God, which is guided by the norm that created perfections must be denied of God, lest God be turned into an idol.

The "divinization" of Christ is in danger of wiping out his humanity and, worse still, of concealing his necessary involvement in the "affairs of this world"—the stage and object of all human conduct. Jesus "went around doing good," but his actions seem so alien to everything that affects our lives that he hardly seems to be one of us at all. The exaltation of his sufferings has also helped to obscure the debates and transactions that are part and parcel of all societal life.

It must be made clear that Jesus, the "assassinated prophet," grappled with the contradictions to be found in the Palestine of his day. He may not have let himself be taken over by any one of the groups or clans that were fighting for power or their version of the truth; but he certainly did not live in isolation from the conflicts dividing his people or from the negotiations that explored the issues. If he himself was not a Zealot, he had Zealots among his disciples; and he also attracted tax collectors, prostitutes, and Pharisees. There have always been some who would like to drape him in a cloak of apoliticism. But underneath any such cloak we can see a rigorous political analysis and praxis, its significance and importance made clear by his condemnation to death.

In this context his stand on the payment of tax tribute to Caesar is of the utmost importance (Matt. 22:15–22; Mark 12:13–17; Luke 20:20–26). Setting a trap for him, the Pharisees and Herodians ask him whether it is permissible to pay taxes to Caesar. That is a political question if there ever was one! His reply was devastating:

> Jesus, aware of their malice, said, "Why put me to the test, you hypocrites? Show me the money for the tax." And they brought him a coin. And Jesus said to them, "Whose likeness and inscription is this?" They said, "Caesar's." Then he said to them, "Render therefore to Caesar the things that are Caesar's, and to God the things that are God's."

This is undoubtedly one of the most misunderstood passages in the gospels. It has been viewed as the basis for making a distinction between authority in "spiritual society" and authority in "temporal society," thus helping to resolve conflicts internal to "Christendom." But the fact is that Jesus says nothing about Caesar's right to receive the tax. Taking note of the fact that it is Caesar who collects it, Jesus directs that the money that is a visible token of Caesar's power be returned to him. But in demanding that tax payers render to God what is God's, Jesus is rejecting Caesar's right to claim what is due to God—that is, worship.

Jesus desacralizes the emperor, reducing him to nothing more than a tax collector. He does not challenge the necessity of taxes for the operation of societal life, or the necessity of some authority charged with the task of collecting them. What he does challenge is that authority's claim to divinity. It is a supremely political act, restoring to societies the authority to organize themselves for the resolution of concrete problems.

The first Christians were not mistaken in their judgment. They were subjects of the law, but dissidents when it came to the worship on which the law was based. They practiced to perfection the principle of clandestine workings, which is the only way to ensure freedom in a totalitarian regime—that is, a sacralized regime. Thus they undermined the very foundations of the system.

Jesus' attitude toward the Jewish law is similar. He reduces it to its proper function: regulating societal life according to the norms arrived at in the course of Israel's creation as God's people. His provocative behavior vis-à-vis the Sabbath points in the same direction. The Sabbath was made to serve human beings, he asserts. His aim is to foster freedom in human evaluation and decision-making so that persons can be active subjects of societal organization rather than passive objects of its processes. Paul the Pharisee would draw the conclusions deriving from that basic stance. At the heart of faith he placed freedom vis-à-vis the law; he himself had been freed from the law by faith.

But it is Jesus' defense of the "rights of the poor" that most clearly brings out his place in the political debate in which he could not help but be involved. In proclaiming the good news of their blessedness to the poor, he was not inviting them to resign themselves to their sad plight and passively wait for the promise of eternal life to be fulfilled. He announced that God was going to put back in order the disorder responsible for their poverty, as we see from his first preaching in Nazareth:

And he came to Nazareth, where he had been brought up; and he went to the synagogue, as his custom was, on the sabbath day. And he stood up to read; and there was given to him the book of the prophet Isaiah. He opened the book and found the place where it was written:

"The spirit of the Lord is upon me,
because he has anointed me
to preach good news to the poor.
He has sent me to proclaim release to the captives
and recovery of sight to the blind,
to set at liberty those who are oppressed,
to proclaim the acceptable year of the Lord."

And he closed the book, and gave it back to the attendant, and sat down; and the eyes of all in the synagogue were fixed on him. And he began to say to them, "Today this scripture has been fulfilled in your hearing." And all spoke well of him, and wondered at the gracious words which proceeded out of his mouth [Luke 4:16–22].

The connection between Jesus' words and the admiration they evoke from his listeners becomes clear only if we see it in terms of the collective consciousness of the Jewish people—that is, the evocation of the Lord's year of grace and the announcement of his coming. We do not know for sure whether the sabbatical year and the Jubilee year ever took real effect in ancient Israel. But the role assigned to them, whether in reality or as a future projection, helped to shape the collective conscience of the nation. The Jews were convinced that some day God would enforce the reoganization of society, a society that had been structured in terms of inequality and injustice. To announce the arrival of that day was to rouse the poor so that they might achieve their rights and fulfil their dreams. It was also to prod them to fashion a world in which their rights would be respected, even though it would take centuries for them to realize that this was the task facing them. Jesus' reply to the emissaries of John the Baptist is in the same vein:

Now when John heard in prison about the deeds of the Christ, he sent word by his disciples and said to him, "Are you he who is to come, or shall we look for another?" And Jesus answered them, "Go and tell John what you hear and see: the blind receive their sight and the lame walk, lepers are cleansed and the deaf hear, and the dead are raised up, and the poor have good news preached to them. And blessed is he who takes no offense at me" [Matt. 11:2–6; cf. Luke 7:8–28].

If the good news proclaimed to the poor did not imply subversion of the established disorder, it would not be such a sign of contradiction. The healing of the sick does not jeopardize societal organization, except perhaps that of the medical profession.

The parable of the good Samaritan (Luke 10:29–37) take up the question of neighborly love in the same vein. Those who place themselves in the service of their fellow human beings are the ones who do what must be done to share in eternal life. Only one task is assigned to Jesus' disciples as their unique law, as the criterion for determining the truth of their relationship to God—namely, building a world in which life is possible. Insofar as human beings find themselves powerless to build such a world, certain tasks become obligatory. And those are the tasks by which God will recognize his own: "Truly, I say to you, as you did it to one of the least of these my brethern, you did it to me" (Matt. 25:40).

Jesus does not propose or expound a political program; his preaching and practice make clear the implications of "love," the one and only law. Insofar as societies cannot achieve justice, insofar as they are unable to elaborate and implement laws and systems that will ensure a fair distribution of necessary goods and services to all, then love excuses no one from taking part in the effort to achieve equality and solidarity. Its function is to make up for the deficiencies and failures of that political practice. Besides finding fulfilment in works of mercy, love is what gives full meaning to relationships between persons; and those interpersonal relationships serve as the sacrament of their relationship with God.

Jesus continues the millennial effort of Israel to link together the construction of society and relationship to God as closely as possible. That effort always seems doomed to failure. It must be taken up anew time and again because societies will be under construction so long as history lasts. But that does not alter the import of Jesus' practice one bit. He fulfils the law by relativizing it so that it may function. His listeners are directed to the tasks of organizing the world on which human existence depends. There can be no question of evading those tasks on the pretext of consecrating oneself to God. God has no desire for a world fashioned to the detriment of the poor, nor does God want worshipers to let such a world develop.

Jesus, then, is at the very heart of the debate about building a world society and defining the connection between that task and recognition of God. His historical situation was different, to be sure. He lived in Palestine when it was occupied by the Romans, when it lay on the periphery of the Roman Empire. Today his followers must transform a system that has subjected the vast majority of humankind to underdevelopment. History does not repeat itself, even though we may find analogies between the two situations. The system being called into question today, for example, grew out of the expansion of medieval Christendom.

We are talking about political tasks when we talk about desacralizing structures that make it impossible for a people to organize itself societally, and about desacralizing a "law" that distracts human beings from their earthly tasks on the pretext of focusing life on the worship of God. The preaching and practice of Jesus make clear, however, that such tasks cannot be dissociated from living our lives in authentic relationship to God. Jesus makes it clear that God is not acknowledged or honored when the rights of the poor are trampled underfoot, when the necessary organization of societal life and divine worship ends up stifling the sovereign liberty of God's children.

The polemical cast of Jesus' attitudes and proposals enables us to grasp the radical nature of the drama in which he was involved. He was concerned about truth as God sees it. The use of God's name to dominate the victims of the system was the supreme example of idolatry in Jesus' eyes. He could not help but reject such a perversion of religion, even though it meant risking his own life. He gave up his life, but he won his battle: three days after his death he was worshiped as Lord, the conqueror of death. In a universe where it was evident that God alone is God, Jesus was raised into the glory of God. He thus was set over against Caesar, who was imposing worship of himself on slaves, and over against the "servants of God" who were using God's law to abet their own privileges.

Himself a victim of those seeking to maintain the existing order, Jesus gathered disciples who dared to act on the promptings of the Spirit. They stood on their own two feet and refused to bow their heads to the imperial idol. Authentic worship of God became possible once again, thus setting in motion the social dynamics that would allow for the ongoing reconstruction of societal structures and relationships.

That historical impetus would again get bogged down in the quicksand of social inertia as Christianity turned into a historical movement. Yet its primal impulses lie buried in the Christian memory, and Christians can go back to these sources and bring them to life once again.

Thesis 23: The work of the fathers of the church vis-à-vis the rights of the poor opens up mystical, ethical, and political perspectives for the shaping of a habitable earth.

Even before Christianity began to spread in Israel and the Roman Empire, even before it began to suffer repression for its religious dissidence, it stepped into history as a utopia put into practice. The Acts of the Apostles and the community memory have preserved the recollection of that utopia, in what is undoubtedly an idealized version:

> And they devoted themselves to the apostles' teaching and fellowship, to the breaking of bread and the prayers. . . . And all who believed were together and had all things in common; and they sold their possessions and goods and distributed them to all, as any had need [Acts 2:42–44].

This effervescent experiment was in full continuity with the preaching of Jesus. It has remained in Christian consciousness as a model of integral communism, and its utopian effects have cropped up repeatedly at critical junctures in church history. The model was impractical, as all utopias are. It functioned for only a short time, and that may have been at the expense of solidarity between the budding communities in the Roman Empire.

Paul's perserverance in taking up a collection for the church at Jerusalem bears witness to the "unrealism" of that adventure on the margins of history. But it must be remembered that the first Christians expected the imminent return of the Lord. They could not imagine an effort to integrate their egalitarianism into a social practice involving active resistance to inequality. By withdrawing from the world they were realizing their "ideal" and thus paving the way for monasticism in all its variety. They thus bore witness to their irreducibility, and to the consistency of their practice with the recognition of God as God and Jesus as Lord.

The church soon spread and took on structured shape. It became part of a society whose sacralized institutions were already in a process of disintegration. We can never offer a final explanation for collective phenomena, and so we shall never be able to say for sure whether the exaltation of Jesus as Lord contributed to the collapse of the existing system. Jesus was certainly set over against Caesar, and Caesar's "divinity" was being called into doubt by the cracks in the imperial system. The social construct based on the exploitation of slaves and conquered provinces was breaking down. Christian churches multiplied and recruited members at every level of society, and their only distinguishing features were rejection of emperor worship and the practice of fraternal communion. The religion of slaves gradually became the religion of patricians and the ruling classes as freedmen or barbarians took over the top posts in the empire.

As the Roman Empire collapsed under a succession of incoherent policies, the church developed its structures along the same lines as those operative in that empire. Thus the contradictions of disintegrating societies were reproduced in the church. It now became a parallel society, and Constantine would put it in charge of the religion of the state.

Two lines of approach would now open up as Christians tried to remain faithful to their original ideal and tried to organize their praxis. Adherents of one approach keenly felt the contradiction between the dynamism embodied in Jesus and societal structuring based on inequality. They headed for the desert, and then to monasteries. They would live out the summons of evangelical radicalism with each other. In asceticism and prayer they would confront the "princes of this world." The other approach was espoused by pastors who were concerned about their responsibilities vis-à-vis the church and the world. Doggedly exploring and interpreting the scriptures, they would formulate norms and structures designed to regulate community life in terms of the rights of the poor.

Destitution could only spread as the imperial system became unhinged, in the West at least. Large towns—vital hubs in the system—were reduced to villages. Land was turned over to soldiers and magistrates in return for their services. Underutilized large estates existed alongside landless peasants. The infrastructure put in place by the legionnaires crumbled, leaving some traces that give us an idea of the organizational work done by Roman jurists and engineers. The ruins give us a hint of what the collapse of an empire means, but they do not serve as well to record the human misery that went hand in hand with opulence in a disintegrating society.

As "everyone" became Christian, Christians themselves got used to those same societal contradictions. They did not mobilize collectively to organize a society that would provide everybody with the basic necessities of life. Those who could accumulate wealth did so, showing little concern for their fellow human beings; and their conduct helped to immerse others deeper in poverty and misery. There were structures that provided for the exercise of charity, for the collection and distribution of goods; but they were no match for the contradictions in a society whose framework was falling apart. The egalitarian thrust of Christianity could find no purchase in the ruins of a commercial economy and its juridical system.

It was against this societal drift that a persistant fight would be waged by pastors, preachers, fathers and doctors of the church. We can find the traces of that fight in a multitude of texts, which should be reread today in the light of our own economic, social, and political history. Confronted with a situation of inequality that gave rise to many injustices, they proclaimed the basic, traditional doctrine in all its radicalness. Though they did not underestimate the necessary tasks of societal management, they stressed communal ownership of goods as the fundamental and traditional principle. The earth belongs to all because everything belongs to God. The poor, as well as the rich, have a right to their proper share inasmuch as all human beings are equal before God.

The fathers of the church elaborated their doctrine in the midst of real-life circumstances, trying to help or persuade Christians to live in accordance with their faith. The primitive communism of the early Christians remained a basic point of reference, though it actually served as a model only for those Christians who withdrew from societal life. The common patristic doctrine was not a systematized theory, nor did it make any claims to be a "social teaching." It took shape around inherited, shared certitudes, which were far from having any decisive impact on de facto practices. The drift of society toward inequality seemed ineluctable. The church fathers basically tried to keep Christians on the alert against that drift. Their work was an effort to negotiate or reduce the contradiction between solidarity based on the recognition of God and the growing gap between rich and poor based on inertial tendencies in society.

Almsgiving is given great stress, so that it might appear to be the main point. But if the duty of almsgiving is hammered home to the rich, it is because a right of the poor is involved. In the case of extreme necessity the poor even have the right to take what they need for survival wherever they find it. In our own day *Populorum Progressio* (n. 23) would reiterate the words of St. Ambrose: "You are not making a gift of what is yours to the poor man, but you are giving him back what is his. You have been appropriating things that are meant to be for the common use of everyone. The earth belongs to everyone, not to the rich."

The church fathers often pinpoint injustice—whether it be usury or the mere accumulation of land and goods—as the source of wealth. More radically, however, they make clear that the basic foundation of any social ethic inspired by Christianity is the principle that the goods of this world are destined for all. Their position is clearly in continuity with the legislative efforts of ancient Israel, the preaching of the ancient prophets, and the message of Jesus. And who can say for sure that they were not consciously carrying out a socio-political practice as well? By virtue of their position, they had a role to play in the effort to resist societal decomposition. And the convergence of their views is so great that it reflects the whole problematic issue of the role of the church in society.

To be sure, they were equally concerned about the eternal salvation of the rich. They knew it was no easy matter, but they did not despair of it. But however much preoccupied with eternal life they may have been, the church fathers were also concerned about easing the temporal plight of the poor. They were anxious to ensure the basic subsistence of the poor even though they could not envision the possibility of helping the poor to organize themselves so that they might move out on their own. In a disintegrating universe the main task was to survive and to prepare as well as one could for eternal life. From that standpoint the rich were in greater danger than the poor.

There is no point in providing a long list of citations here. Various anthologies of patristic writings are available, and A. Hamman has edited a collection of texts about the rich and the poor in the early Church (*Riches et pauvres dans l'Eglise ancienne*, Grasset, 1962; see also Charles Avila, *Ownership: Early Cristian Teaching*, Maryknoll, N.Y.: Orbis Books, 1983). I shall simply cite one text of Gregory the Great (sixth century), italicizing key words. It makes clear, I think, that the obligation to share goods derives from justice rather than from charitable promptings. The text comes from his *Regulae pastoralis liber*:

> Different reproof must be meted out to those who do not commit *thefts* but fail to *give alms,* and those who give *charity* out of their own fortune but do not stop *stealing the goods of others*. The first group must be made to realize clearly that *this earth* from which they were drawn is *common to all human beings;* hence *the provisions furnished by it are for all in common*. Those are wrong who protest their innocence when they *take over for their private use the gift that God made for all*. If they do not give alms out of the goods they have received, they become *guilty of the death of their fellow human beings*. Insofar as they avariciously withhold necessities from the poor who are dying of hunger, they let them perish. When we supply necessities to fill their needs, we are not indulging in personal generosity; *we are giving them back what belongs to them*. We are fulfilling a *duty of justice* rather than performing an act of charity. Truth itself had this to say by way of explaining the obligation of practicing mercy wisely: "Beware of doing your *justice* before human beings." To this may be added the words of the psalmist . . . about the just person: "He sows alms, he gives to the needy, his justice is forever." After mentioning charity to the poor, then, the sacred author chose the word "justice" for it. . . . It is only just and right that those who have received something from God, the common master, should use it for the welfare of all. Hence Solomon's maxim: "The just give without respite" [Migne, P.L., 77/3/XXI, c. 87].

Pope Gregory juggles words to point up obligations that should be obvious but that have hardly any real impact on societal life. His effort only highlights the fact that Christianity is not so much a theory as a practice. It is not an endless effort to articulate *all the truths* of faith so much as it is a practice guided by *one norm:* active resistance to the inevitable structuring of societies in terms of inequality. That is the point made in Christian doctrine, of course. But in the last analysis it is the doing that counts. Christianity is a historical movement, not a system of ideas.

Chapter 6

The Perversion and Renaissance of Christianity

In order to gain access to the highpoints of its praxis in past history, the church must look closely at the long period when Christianity was perverted into Christendom. It must heed and accept the criticism made of that period; such criticism is necessary. But then it must try to move beyond that criticism, in the effort to get back to its original, theoretical truth. Critical analysis is a requirement if the church is to elucidate and implement a praxis that would restore Christianity to life as a historical movement in which God comes to be recognized as the liberator of the poor and oppressed.

Thesis 24: In becoming the "civil religion" of the West, Christianity for a long time lost its ability to effectively resist the structuring of societies in terms of inequality.

We do not know for sure whether Christianity abetted the disintegration of the Roman Empire by desacralizing its setup. What is certain is that Christianity did spread by means of the administrative and commercial networks of the empire. Making use of existing structures, which provided some degree of coherence, the church had time to grow and organize. Coordination and unity were ensured to some extent by the system of dioceses, with their links to archdioceses, patriarchates, and the papacy. This spatial organization and interrelationship was reinforced further from the sixth century onward by growing networks of interconnected monasteries.

Christianity became the dominant religion, and it would be embraced by the "barbarians" whose invasions had disrupted the old imperial system. It thus became a unifying force in a situation where no other organization could ensure functional cohesion. Over the course of ensuing centuries Christianity would undergo a change. Later critical analysis of that change would see it as a perversion or distortion of Christianity's prehistory and original dynamics. At its start Christianity had been a force resistant to the structuring of societies in terms of inequality. It now became a force sacralizing societies that were organized rigidly in terms of inequality. Christianity—or the church system that embodied it—became the official religion: a point of reference and a seat of ideological power. The civil power had to take it into account. Indeed the civil power was dependent on it for its stability and functioning.

Let us focus briefly on the period when centralized states were established. Various forms of fragile balance came into existence, based on a distinction between the role of "temporal power" and "spiritual power." The image of the empire as the antithesis of pervasive disorder would center around the papacy and the system organized around it. Efforts to restore the old Roman order would never go beyond the enthronement of an "outsider" emperor, who would receive his mandate symbolically from the "insider" emperor: the pope. Imperial succession in the West would be organized and conducted by the pope and the church. The old Roman emperors had become divine in order to rule. Their successors would now have to deny their divinity in order to fill their shoes, with God's backing. But God was now in danger of being made the guardian of the new order that had to be built out of the ruins of a disorganized society.

The disorder resulting from the progressive disintegration of the Roman Empire in the West made security the chief preoccupation of every human group. The migrations of peoples through Europe inevitably led to conflicts between them. Basic organization became a requirement for survival. Only then could anyone dream of fleshing out the other structures necessary for societal life.

In such a situation the warriors, those who defended the territory of a given group, tended to take over the top posts of social power and responsibility. All others had to rely on them; everything depended on their efforts. The warriors became princes and kings, imposing their authority on those who had formerly been their peers and electors. The ruins of castles and fortresses bear witness to the slow reorganization of Europe and its recovery from anarchy. In certain areas we can still find vivid reminders of the older Roman infrastructure. Societal restructuring necessarily entailed sacralization of the new relationships between various human groups and their representative leaders. The baptism of Clovis and the coronations of Pepin and Charlemagne would lead to social and mental structures that would be normative for a millennium. The oath of fealty and vassalage indicate that feudal social relationships were modeled after the individual's relationship to God.

Even though the ambitions of churchmen may not have been out of tune with this whole process, it arose out of historical necessity. Warriors and princes were often unable to guarantee security. Indeed they intensified the feeling of insecurity by encroaching upon neighboring territories in order to defend their own. Death was everywhere. Persons were continually in danger of dying from physical violence, hunger, and disease. Economic activity might be reduced to the production of the barest necessities. Plagues and epidemics could be spread by roving warriors, traveling merchants, and pilgrims.

With death an ever-present menace, eternal life was the only prospect that offered real security. The church held the key to that possibility, so that it became the real locus of human lives. Preparing for a happy death became the main concern. The defenseless had no other hope. Economic and military leaders could not help but incur guilt in their enterprises, so they were forced to submit to the church, its norms, and its organizational structure. A religion of eternal salvation took shape and held sway for a long time, reinforcing the sacralization of a social system based upon the submission of princes to priests. As is true in every relationship of dependence and domination, the priests became the allies of the princes. When the princes managed to consolidate their power, the church found itself enfeoffed. Like the masses, the church had need of the order they were establishing.

Over the course of centuries the network of dioceses and monasteries became the warp and woof of the fabric of society. At the start they had been the agents of societal reorganization. They ended as integral parts of the system they had helped to build and sacralize. The appointment of abbots and bishops by king and emperor was a logical outcome of this interdependence, and it was only natural for Napoleon Bonaparte to think of "his" bishops as he did of his prefects.

We should not pass judgment lightly on this perversion of Christianity. It is true that Christianity was gradually transformed into the civil religion of the West, now organized as Christendom, whereas it originally had been a movement of a different sort. This perversion came about in the confrontation with harsh historical necessities. It was helped along by commonplace certitudes inherited from the Roman Empire and by the functioning of church structures that served as models for the societal structures that had to be established.

On the other hand we should not try to overlook or conceal the role of the church in the development of the West either. Out of that development would come the underdevelopment of the rest of the world. The church served to sacralize the system, to offer the religious representations that made it seem natural and right.

That was not the only role played by the church, however. To reduce it to the "ideological apparatus of the state" would be to indulge in historical oversimplification. It may well have helped to legitimate established authorities by anointing rulers. But throughout the period from the sixth to the sixteenth century it also tried to correct the effects and excesses of a social organization based on the domination of the common people by rulers and noblemen. The church prayed for the dead, but it did not limit itself to preaching resignation to a harsh earthly life and submission to one's rulers and defenders. In varying degrees of consistency and effectiveness it also tried to ensure that the poor and needy would get the goods and services to which they had a right. When the teachings of the church fathers were kept alive, some persons would take sides with the poor and try to serve them out of loyalty to the gospel. As the research of Michel Mollat makes clear (*Les pauvres au Moyen Age*, Paris: Hachette, 1978), we cannot ignore the immense organizational effort of social welfare that went hand in hand with the church's sacralization of the established medieval order.

Viewing those efforts from our own standpoint in the twentieth century, as we try to explore the role of the church in the development of peoples and the transformation of the prevailing system, we cannot help but be struck by the ineffectiveness of the church's corrective measures. Indeed was it even possible for the medieval church to overcome the contradiction in which it was involved? On the one hand it gave legitimation to the medieval social order. On the other hand it had to keep increasing its palliative efforts, due to the inequities and injustices produced by the maldistribution of resources, tasks, and responsibilities.

The "religious factor" became an even weightier social factor from the seventh century on when another religion turned into an effective social force. Islam began to conquer and reorganize the southern Mediterranean, spreading east into Asia. Even before they confronted each other in the Crusades, the two socio-religious systems were mutually influencing one another. Both were engaged in reappropriating the thought and normative systems of antiquity. Both were articulating the connection between warrior authorities and religious norms for the regulation of community life. When the moment of confrontation came, crusades would be organized to win back the Holy Land and the Holy Sepulcher in the context of feuds between European princes. This only reinforced the hold of the church on societal life, and its dependence on the established order.

Such was the logic of the involvement of religion in societal structures and relationships. Protests and ruptures were bound to surface at some point. As the system solidified and spread around the world, individuals were bound to ask what the gospel message and divine worship really meant. In becoming the religion of an expanding civilization that threatened every other civilization, Christianity was exposing itself to the risk of dying, as might any civilization.

For a long time, however, the Christendom model prevailed and was identified with the church. It gave rise to its own mental and symbolic structuration. We still face the urgent and necessary task of dismantling or deconstructing that model if we wish to engage in political thought and action in our present world. It may be a post-Christian world, but only because it is organized on the ruins of an older Christendom.

Thesis 25: In failing to become the civil religion of the world that was being reorganized in European terms, Christianity regained its chance to represent the poor and their hopes.

Becoming the civil religion of the West, Christianity was inevitably enmeshed in the European colonial adventure and its disorganizing and reorganizing effects on the rest of the world. Upholding the ideals, values, and symbolic interests of Christendom, along with their economic and political counterparts, the church legitimated the conquest of the world by defining its objective: the evangelization of newly discovered peoples. And this was done even before it was sure that they were human.

By the Treaty of Tordesillas (1493), which divided the non-Christian world into Spanish and Portuguese spheres of influence, Pope Alexander VI tried to ensure papal control over the process of colonization. The *patronato* delegated extensive authority to the Iberian rulers in the transplanting of church structures. But Christendom would soon splinter under the impact of the Reformation.

The great missionary journeys of the thirteenth century, which followed the routes of merchants and explorers as far as China, had had no colonial overtones. By contrast the great missionary impulse of the sixteenth century was caught up in a twofold logic: resisting and bypassing Islam and seeking conquests for the sake of gold, spices, and slaves. The whole venture was economic and political, first of all, even though the proclamation of the gospel was used to legitimate it. Is it simple chance or coincidence that the departure of Columbus took place the very same year in which Granada was regained from the Muslims, thus completing the recovery of the Iberian peninsula? That struggle, which had turned into a confrontation between two worlds as well as two religions, would be carried on in the race for world domination.

It was not just the church made up of the faith and its sacraments that was transplanted. It was, even more perhaps, Christendom as a hierarchial and sacralized system of social relationships. Newly discovered peoples were baptized, to be sure, often without any real evangelization beforehand; but they were also subjected to hard labor in mines and plantations. Europe was greedy for gold and exotic products. It needed goods and currency for the development of its mercantile economy. A triangular trade pattern would soon bring manufactured goods from Europe to Africa, slaves from Africa to the Americas, and cotton and coffee from the Americas to Europe.

Seasonal winds and ocean currents might suggest to some that these organized trade routes were inscribed in the very nature of things. It was as if divine providence had ordained civilized Christians to carry out the task of evangelizing and civilizing other peoples living in darkness and the shadow of death. Even in recent times the two tasks were associated in the official language of the church, suggesting how much they were taken for granted as parts of one and the same enterprise. In Christendom it was taken for granted that the "kingdom of Christ" had taken over the role of the old Roman Empire.

Ethnocide and genocide, provoked by this assurance of the truth, were the most glaring effects of this "totalitarian Christianity" (Delumeau), though they were often kept well hidden. The wars of religion that rent Europe, even as that continent was imposing its domination on the rest of the world, were another sample of the "religious" passion that was then involved in organizing relationships between human groups and nations. The barbarity of other peoples was obvious to the recently civilized Europeans. The elimination of barbarity fitted in perfectly with the European concept of a "holy war." In their clash with the Muslims, Europeans had reproached them for the slogan "Believe or die!" Now Europeans could address the same slogan to their new-found "savages."

During the reconstruction of Europe the church had done little more than attempt to correct the defects and injustices of the system it was legitimating by offering palliative measures. Now, however, churchmen and gospel witnesses arose in the church to challenge the system of domination or its forms of implementation. They focused on the proclamation of the good news of Jesus Christ, the goal that the popes had assigned to the colonial enterprise. This led them to confront the authorities in power, to act as fierce defenders of the rights of peoples. Bartolomé de Las Casas (1474–1566), the most famous representative of this long-forgotten breed, did not hesitate to subordinate evangelization itself to the right of a people to follow its own path. "Better a live pagan Indian than a dead Christian Indian." Aided by his Dominican confrères at Salamanca, and especially the theologian Francisco de Vitoria (d. 1546), Las Casas would break new ground for international law and human rights.

The fact that this intrepid defender of the Indians went so far as to approve of the black slave trade, though he publicly repented of this before he died, indicates that the evangelization of peoples does not necessarily entail recognition of their humanity. The "black legend" banished Las Casas from his people's memory for centuries, suggesting how much his fight went against the collective certitudes of Christendom: its conviction that it had the truth as well as a right and a duty to "civilize" other nations.

Las Casas's fight was lost in the end. The expulsion of the Jesuits from Latin America in the eighteenth century put an end to the organized defense of the Indians. His evangelical firmness would not surface again in the collective conscience of society and church until the close of the colonial era (Bandung, 1955; Algiers, 1973). But it stands in history as the first break in the Christendom system, where divine worship was subordinated to the sacralization of social organization instead of keeping it under control.

My point is not to use the example of Las Casas for apologetics. He and his fellow fighters were defeated, after all. The transplantation of Christendom and the disorganization of traditional civilizations and societies went on. But it is important to remember his fight if we are to appreciate the potential role of the church in the development of peoples.

The imposition of Christendom structures was an integral part of colonization, but it entailed the birth of churches in the colonized lands. After centuries of dependence—economic, political, social, cultural, and theological—they would surface in the universal church as "churches of the poor, born of the people." They could once again hear and heed the good news proclaimed to the poor insofar as they were caught up in the liberation movements of their own peoples. They were on the periphery of the church, as their societies were on the periphery of the world system. In the socio-cultural locale constituted by the church, they were starting points for a rediscovery of the gospel message with all its radical political import as the word of God.

While the church continued to be bogged down in the Christendom pattern, a rebirth of Christianity began to take place. It was a revival of the praxis of the Hebrew legislators and prophets, of Jesus and the church fathers. This time, however, the implications of Jesus' message were made explicit. The poor themselves discovered their rights as they listened to the good news addressed to them, and they set out to turn those rights into realities. In the very process of liberation they came to realize that it was God who was summoning them to stand tall and take charge of their own history.

The way was being paved for this movement throughout the colonial period by the passive resistance of the colonized peoples to the norms, rites, and representations imposed upon them from the outside. The movement itself, with its roots buried deeply in history and the collective memory, has again come face to face with the certitudes of Christendom that blocked the appeals of Las Casas in an earlier day. We do not know for sure whether the modern awakening of the Indian will be Christian or not, but it does mark the long-term victory of those who have defended the rights of the poor in God's name. In their congresses and parliaments the oppressed now honor the memory of their many defenders over the centuries.

There is much food for thought in all this, at least for those who believe that Christianity has historical relevance when it remains true to its main thrust and identifies the defense of the poor with recognition of God. When the vanquished speak up and challenge the views imposed on them by their conquerors, it is as if Christianity had passed through death to new life. It is the power of God clearly at work in history once again.

The persecution of these "new Christians" by the established authorities, who claim to be defending "Christian civilization," is one more indication that their confession of faith is in continuity with that of the first Christians. The socio-religious dissidence of the first Christians came down to refusing to worship Caesar, because Jesus had said that such worship belonged to God alone. If the universal church is to gauge the full import of such martyrdom, it must finish the task of dismantling the inherited certitudes of Christendom that equate the "maintenance of order" with the defense of "God's rights."

Las Casas's fight will go on so long as the church continues to harbor nostalgia for Christendom as it was conceived in the romantic or neo-Gothic dreams of nineteenth-century postrevolutionary restorations. Rearguard maneuvers continue to paralyze the inner life of the church. They indicate how difficult it is to go back to the sources of sacred history and the gospel message, which are far too subversive for the little princes who dream of serving the masses and making them happy in spite of themselves.

New pathways are opening up for the church, pathways carved out in the spirit of those who were defeated in the sixteenth century. But they will lead to glory only insofar as they are filled with suffering as well. They are seedbeds waiting for the blood of martyrs.

Thesis 26: When God is transformed into the guardian of an established order, atheism seems to be a prerequisite for social change.

When Jesus, a victim to the maintenance of order, was worshiped as Lord, the divinity of Caesar soon became a joke. But when the God of Jesus became the keystone of a new empire, the basic preconditions for his rejection were at hand. Viewed from this standpoint, modern atheism is a historical necessity. It takes up the fight of Jesus and his Hebrew predecessors against the sacralization of authorities who organize society in terms of inequality and injustice. Because the negation of God opens the way for the enthronement of new deities, modern atheism will give rise to its own contradiction. Indeed we see that process already at work in the spiritual resistance to various forms of totalitarianism.

The Judeo-Christian tradition entrusted the world to a humanity created in the image and likeness of God. It thus paved the way for a collective effort to master nature and history. The basic orientation and import of this effort was provided by divine revelation. The world was created by a God who is "wholly different" from that created world. If God is God, then nothing in this world is sacred. Everything in it has been entrusted to human beings. They fashion themselves into humanity by ordering all things to achieve the basic goal that keeps them united.

A limitless field was opened up for rational effort. Human beings could investigate and master nature in all its forms, as if God did not exist (Bonhoeffer), and they were obliged to do so. Of necessity and by vocation humankind was a demiurge, empowered and obliged to transform the world and take charge of its own history. The desacralization of Caesar gave back the power to organize societal life and relationships in such a way that goods and services might be produced to satisfy the basic needs of all.

It was almost inevitable that the course of rational investigation, designed to provide humans with a firm grasp of reality, should lead to atheism. The approach itself implied "methodological atheism," and it is difficult for human beings to attain the wisdom that would relativize every effort to achieve total knowledge.

Every developing science seems to tend toward scientism. If scientism soon proves to be ridiculous, it nevertheless seems bound to occur so long as the limits and weaknesses of new and obvious explanations do not surface clearly. Thus atheism, the questioning of God's existence, seems to flow naturally from a rational process that has become rationalistic.

Certain questions could not be raised as long as the imaginary ideal of truth held sway. Those questions now raise anxious concern in all those who try to account for their relationship with the God who still guides or determines their lives. The vulnerability of the believing conscience vis-à-vis that atheism is just as respectable as the serenity of those who have learned to live as if God did not exist.

It is not that particular brand of atheism, however, that has had the most radical effect on the history of the past few centuries. More important has been the atheism required to allow for needed social transformations in a world where burgeoning social classes were replacing the religious orders or states of life that had structured Christendom. When society was organized by those who prayed for the dead and those who ensured its defense, the laboring population could work in peace even though peace was never a sure thing. Then the laboring classes discovered from experience that adequate organization of collective life depended on their access to the power once reserved to priests and princes. The old system of power and authority had to be dismantled and then reconstructed to serve the needs and requirements of a soundly organized social system.

Men of God had been anointing the kings who stood at the apex of the existing social hierarchy. To remove the obstacles to needed social changes, it was necessary to desacralize rulers and the system they symbolized by denying the divinity of the God whose lieutenants they were.

This societal effort to regain the power needed for societal self-reproduction took shape gradually between the sixteenth and eighteenth centuries. It ended up in the philosophy of the Enlightenment and Marxist atheism. Yet it is not unlike the millennial effort of ancient Israel and the church to prevent divine worship from legitimating a society whose dynamics were geared to benefit ruling minorities. This needed desacralization of the social system joined with the methodological atheism of the scientific method to produce a political atheism. Its pertinence seems to be obvious. Indeed the secularization of societies and the "death of God" are now so taken for granted that even followers of Jesus would prefer to enter politics without worrying too much about the God in whose name Jesus challenged Caesar.

In such a context those Christians who become Marxists and go all the way to atheism seem to be more consistent than those who adopt a Marxist analysis but rule out atheism. The latter seem to overlook the fact that Marxism is not a "tool box" but a revolutionary praxis, its real starting point being the desacralization and destabilization of a system built upon inequality and injustice. The Marxist process would become insignificant if it excluded atheism.

The real unanswered question is whether the Marxist approach will prove in the long run to be more useful in effecting the needed revolutions than will a Christian approach that gets back to its original praxis and sees the fight for justice as inextricably bound up with its recognition of God as God. So long as the church's trajectory is not reoriented around the main thrust of the Judeo-Christian heritage, there will be no point in trying to hide or forbid the drift of militant Christians, aware of the need to change the world, toward a revolutionary praxis defined in Marxist terms.

The real issue at stake in the competition between Christianity and Marxism is how we are to construct a world society that will ensure a more equitable distribution of necessary goods and services to all human beings. So long as the church does not tackle this issue and organize itself to assume its proper role in this effort, its resistance to Marxism will be as meaningless as the debates of Byzantine theologians over the sex of angels when the Turks were at the gates. If the church does organize and mobilize to change the world, on the other hand, it will be in a position to meet the challenge now posed. It will then be possible to verify whether atheism is more effective for the transformation of the world than is an acknowledgment of God that entails fighting for justice.

The question of God's existence is not really the issue at the core of the present debate. The key issue is the ability of Christians to work for true human progress. The seeming contradiction between worship of God and the shaping of the world is silly and illusory, but it still paralyzes the church. So long as that contradiction is not surmounted, there is a danger that Christianity will become increasingly irrelevant for those who take seriously the life of human beings and the future of humanity.

It is no accident that we find the negation of God associated with revolution. The association became necessary insofar as the church was caught up in the task of sacralizing a system whose deleterious effects it did not even notice. Revolution was necessary, and it could take place only by denying the very basis of the church's ideological power.

Modern atheism is the product of the emancipation of post-Christian societies from the tutelage that had been imposed on them by the church. Social organizations inevitably undergo sacralization; they must be desacralized when they become inadequate. This produces contradictions, and modern atheism is the historical effect of the way those contradictions were negotiated in the West. It is now a historical datum that must be taken into account. Whether we regret it or not, it was the condition for getting societies moving. Now that such societal movement is a fact, we can actually envision the construction of societies that will be more just. Implementing various means of investigation and organization, society can now work on restructuring itself.

The methodical structuring of societal and international relationships was once the task of a select few. The vast majority of human beings knew little about it, and often they were hurt by it. Now that task is potentially the task of all. All can participate in it to some extent, even if that means no more than checking on the work done by those who claim divine delegation of leadership and realizing that they are not infallible, as they might have us believe. So long as "new gods" are not foisted on us, the pathways now open for understanding and mastering societal self-production can truly be pathways of freedom.

Although this historical movement has been carried out in opposition to Christianity, or on its margins, it is now clear that it offers Christianity a chance to rediscover itself and take on new life as a historical movement. Criticism of religion was a necessary phase in the revolution. Undoubtedly it was also the most beneficial "historical accident" in the history of Christianity since Christianity got caught up in the toils of Christendom. It is not that it has led to the replacement of religion by faith, as if faith in God were areligious. Rather, it has confronted the church with the obligation to rediscover the exigencies of authentic religion; and those exigencies come down to identifying worship of God with the fight for justice.

Whether the wise agree or not, God can be a more formidable and effective force for the transformation of the world than can the denial of God and the consequent exaltation of human nature. God, creator of creators and liberator of those liberating themselves from oppression and societal stagnation, can cause the most sacralized empires to tremble and totter. It is easy to understand why those who rule the world are not always displeased to see church personnel wasting their time and energy in "theological" disputes. After all, that is the way they describe their own arguments when they do not seem to have anything to do with the real tasks at hand.

Atheism, a historical necessity, could well pave the way for the return of God. And God's return could upset the present equilibrium of society just as much as the denial of God did when God had become the guardian of the established order.

Thesis 27: A critical reading of church history is a precondition for Christianity to have a fresh start as a historical movement.

Christians, and Catholics especially, are so used to viewing the church as their mother and teacher (*Mater et Magistra*) that every attempt to engage in a critical-minded reading of its history or practice initially meets with denial and rejection. That reaction is all the stronger insofar as it is often unacknowledged.

It must be admitted that for several centuries, and for several decades within the Catholic Church itself, the church has been exposed to a negative, corrosive, and sometimes malevolent type of criticism. This was not unconnected with the role that the church had played in earlier history. The effects of that role, as perceived or experienced by flesh-and-blood persons, left wounds that had never healed. The scars of the French Revolution evident in certain churches or their ruins bear witness to the rage and resentment that found retaliatory expression.

Nevertheless ecclesiastical resistance to critical self-analysis must be surmounted, as must the fear of confronting the church. That is the condition that must be met if truth is to come to light. Even more importantly, it is the condition that must be met if we are to build a church whose presence will be relevant in the process of history now at work—that is, by injecting into it the dynamism of the gospel message, the word of God at work in the creation and transformation of the world.

Christianity arose out of a critical-minded reading of history, and more specifically, of the distortions produced by efforts at societal regulation in the Old Testament period. From the very start, therefore, Christianity was a protest movement challenging any and all practical results that contradicted "the way"; and its "way" was defined in terms of the acknowledgment of God as God. Jesus confronted Caesar, his imperial order based on slavery, the guardians of the Jewish law, and even the law itself. With a strictness that could not help but be polemical, he presented himself as the supreme witness to the fact that there is no master for us but God, that we are free from every idol and every system of domination. Although he was indulgent of weakness, he strongly opposed the conceited self-sufficiency of those who wished to impose their ideas on others as the norm, all the more because their words were often in contradiction with their deeds. Those who were liberated by their faith in him, who went to their death rather than bow to an idol, were not fanatic advocates of an ideology or a cause. They were witnesses to the freedom of God's children. For them only God, in unspeakable transcendence, was beyond all criticism, remaining above and beyond any and every representation that we might fashion of God.

We must go back to the very roots of the faith in history if we want to live it today by critically confronting the distortions that were bound to occur in its communal interpretation and practice. The church is assured of the guidance of the Spirit on its journey. Hence it, more than any other organization, is in a position to submit itself to the critical analysis that becomes possible for humanity when it acquires the methods and disciplines permitting rational investigation into what is confronted in the ongoing process of humanization. Just as humanity has overcome nature and the rigidity of its own production routines, so the church is called to move beyond its successive embodiment in various forms of Christendom.

The church is itself only to the extent that it engages in ongoing self-criticism, continually questioning and transcending the formulations and concrete embodiments of the faith that it worked out in the past. More time is needed for the truth of this certainty to get across, particularly because human groups cannot remain permanently in a state of ferment. But at this critical juncture in its history the church will be itself only when it accepts that certainty. Only then will real updating be possible. Only then will it move from mere "housecleaning" to a radical examination of structures and dynamic processes. This will demand the thoughtful attention to which the lowly who believe in God are entitled. It will also demand rigorous analysis. That is what those in power are "entitled to," because wittingly or unwittingly they continually try to expropriate the ideological power and authority of the church for their own benefit.

There is an irresistible tendency to inject into our analyses of structures the aspirations, utopian dreams, and projections that went into them. What is needed, however, is rigorousness in our analyses. Without it we cannot really discover or explain the mechanisms or patterns of nature or societal life. As is true in the case of social dynamics, the subjective intentions of church representatives must be excluded from our analysis, for the simple reason that they are inaccessible to us. We must try to understand what has actually taken place in history, not what could or should have taken place. We must try to understand practices and their correlations, not intentions. Even the practices of duly canonized saints must be subjected to the glaring light of rigorous probing. Our aim is to gain the understanding we need to guide societal practices in a more satisfactory way.

What we are hoping for is a collective "definition" of the roles and tasks that the church might perform in the transformation of the world. But that will be possible only if the church is truly willing to analyze the roles it has played in the past, the tasks it has undertaken, the effects it has produced, and the structures it has imposed on itself. Remember that the church, more than any other organization, is inclined to think that its structures are constitutive of its very reality. Indeed the church is the very prototype of a basic tendency found in every society: the tendency to sacralize structures as they take shape. Critical examination of this tendency is undoubtedly a part of any effort to dismantle systems that have become locked into the assumption that their nature is self-evident.

If the present organization of the world is to be laid bare in such a way that effective transformation becomes possible, the church must be willing to shed light on the roles it has played in fashioning and sacralizing it. The fact that the church has been exposed to this criticism from the outside for a long time does not dispense it from the obligation of assimilating that criticism into its own praxis.

It is, at bottom, the church's embodiment in Christendom that it must subject to full-scale historical, economic, sociological, political, *and* theological investigation. When the social system hallowed as Christendom underwent worldwide expansion, it had an enormous and terrible impact on the history of other peoples and nations. Those responsible for that process must be willing to analyze what it produced, not what its intentions were.

The church really has no reason to fear such an investigation. There are already many indications that it would restore to the church its original élan and vivacity. Collective fear of the truth may not yet be overcome, but the theological fruitfulness of a critical-minded ecclesiology has already become evident.

Building on its Old Testament prehistory, the gospel message laid the theoretical foundations for resisting the sacralization of social organizations. As history turned out, however, it served to establish and sacralize one of the most "successful" theocracies ever known. All power and authority was viewed as emanating from God, through the mediation of the church. This perversion must be pointed up clearly and then eradicated if history is to move on to the radical transformation of existing social systems. That has not yet happened, because the nations that were once Christians are still reluctant to make the necessary moves.

The difficulty of this critical task is further aggravated by the fact that it must be undertaken by the church as a corporate body, not just by observers and analysts, if it is to be truly effective. The road is being paved by militants and activist minorities. Already committed to the struggle for development, they want to get the church truly involved as well. As their numbers grow and they make their voice heard in the church, even in its official pronouncements, they help set in motion the needed investigation of underdevelopment and its causes. Every opening must be explored so that we can utilize as many approaches as possible in our efforts to transform the system.

The responsibility of the church to undertake analysis is brought out all the more clearly by the fact that in some places public authorities appeal to the image of Christendom to reject policies designed to foster development. This does not mean that the church must necessarily go back and redo economic, sociological, and political studies of the mechanisms that must be overhauled. Instead it must link them up with God and God's plan for the world. It must explore its collective memory once again and rediscover its original praxis of actively resisting the formation and sacralization of societies based on inequality and injustice. It must rediscover its formative tradition, in which the acknowledgment of God and the struggle for justice are inextricably linked. We find this linkage rediscovered and expressed in the document of the 1971 Synod of Bishops: "Action on behalf of justice and participation in the transformation of the world fully appear to us as a constitutive dimension of the preaching of the gospel, or, in other words, of the church's mission for the redemption of the human race and its liberation from every oppressive situation" (n.6). If this perception has evoked such a welcome response in churches already involved in the liberation movement, and much resistance elsewhere, it is because it brought out one of the features of ecclesial identity that has long been buried in the obscure recesses of the church's memory.

But talk is not enough, even when it is to the point. It is practice that matters. If that practice is both analytical and enterprising, it will astound both the world and the church itself. Indeed that practice is already underway wherever Christians realize what is at stake and settle down to the tasks on which world development depends. Those Christians know that priority must be given to the reconstruction of disintegrated societies and the construction of a world society; but they also know, or sense, that in carrying out that task they are also building up the church. It is now time to coordinate their efforts, and to provide the theoretical framework that will explain and justify the way they are living out their faith.

Providing a theoretical framework is a properly theological task, which must be carried out as fully and rigorously as possible. It means that the whole church must devote itself to a critical analysis of the totalitarianism embodied in sacralized Christendom. By comparison with that obligatory task, much of the church's present talk is impoverished, insignificant, and aggressively self-defensive. It gives the impression that what is theoretically possible and necessary for Christianity is historically impossible for the church. But to believe in the Spirit is also to believe in the real ability of the church to submit to the truth that must be put into practice.

Chapter 7

Operative Concepts for Analyzing and Transforming the World

When the church probes its collective memory, analyzing and criticizing its own history, it finds in its own language certain concepts and mental constructs that enable it to apprehend and go to work on social reality. We shall consider three basic concepts in this chapter.

Thesis 28: Because the world is structured in sin, participation in its transformation becomes a necessary condition for conversion to God in Jesus Christ.

Taking up and extending the various economic, sociological, and political analyses of the present industrial system and its inability to provide worldwide development for humanity, the church carries to its limit the ultimate ethical judgment on the radical injustice of this world. The church is prompted to analyze in strictly theological terms, the present world as a sinful world, as a world structured in sin. In short, it is a world in contradiction with God, with the plan of God. To resign itself to a world order that necessarily entails underdevelopment, injustice, and poverty would be incompatible with the acknowledgment of God as God, of God as revealed in Jesus Christ.

If the theological concept of sin is to function adequately in the church's analysis of reality, we must carefully differentiate the elements in it without, of course, dissociating them.

Originally the concept had the basic meaning of being in contradiction with God, with the plan or will of God. It signified a distortion in a human being's relationship with God. Revelation unveils a God who has a plan for the world. Certainly that much is implied in the notion that the human being is created in God's image and likeness. But a world shaped in such a way that most of humanity suffers from famine, poverty, and impotence can hardly be in harmony with God's plan. Although God proposes the ideal of fulfillment and communion in the divine image and likeness, God does not provide a ready-made model of how it is to be accomplished. However, God does provide a frame of reference for evaluating what takes place in history. What has taken place in the process of world industrialization and forced unification clearly contradicts God's plan. To defend that process we must either deny God or use God as justification for the way things are because the results suit us.

The denial and rejection of God did take place: it was a necessary prerequisite for the way the world was to be tranformed. Nothing was gained by that denial, however, because there soon came a proliferation of false gods. And their machinations proved to be even more alienating than the use to which the true God had been put.

It gradually came to be realized that acknowledgment of God demands the transformation of the world. The present world situation is clearly incompatible with anything we might say in God's name, and that fact has to be brought out. Thanks to atheism, or in spite of it, some believers have discovered that God is summoning them to save themselves from this sinful world—not by fleeing it but by participating in its transformation. God proves to be a radical, subversive protester.

If we really want to make clear the contradiction between de facto history and the design of God, we must set aside the whole question of the intentions and personal accountability of the makers of history. History is not made by their intentions but by their practices. And those practices intertwine in all sorts of unforeseeable and haphazard ways. Advances in critical analysis enable us to envision the regulation and rectification of societal dynamics, but there is no question of our taking into account the intentions of individuals or groups who have made history. It is what has actually happened in history that must be evaluated, our aim being to set straight the orientations and mechanisms of societal life while it is still possible.

In delineating the concept of sin, we must also disregard and set aside the fatalistic determinations evoked by the idea or myth of original sin. It is not that it is meaningless or unimportant. The simple fact is that this anthropological datum of divine revelation emphasizes the radicalness of salvation, thereby ruling out pessimism and despair. If we refer to it as a "happy fault" that leads to a superabundance of grace, it is because it opens up a horizon for humanity rather than locking us up in our misfortune. Although we do not want to erase this aspect of the human mystery, we must set it aside in fashioning our concept of the sinfulness of the world. Why? Because we are looking for an operative concept that will be useful in our analysis, an analysis designed to make possible the freely chosen transformation of the world.

Our concept of the sinfulness of the world brings out certain distortions in the conduct of history, and those distortions appear to be historical accidents. Whether they were inevitable or not, the opposition of Bartolomé de Las Casas and others like him suggests that what actually took place was not taken for granted as inevitable by all. So *a posteriori* we can interpret sequences of events in terms of the truth, which points up distortions and perversions as it comes to light, rather than in terms of the apparent certainties created by historical events.

Despite all the precautions noted above, it is still possible that a critical analysis of history based on the concept of sin may give rise to feelings of guilt. Such feelings may prompt some to resist any such critical analysis of history, may undermine the will to change things. I would make only two points here. First, when properly handled, guilt feelings can serve as the starting point for action. Secondly, it is the role of the church to help its members handle their guilt feelings as well as they can.

It is also possible that some might be suspicious about the church's motives in talking about the sinfulness of the world. They might fear that it is trying to regain or consolidate its power over consciences, inasmuch as it has "the power to forgive sins." Realistic appreciation of this fear and suspicion should enable the church to eliminate every hint of magic from its sacramental practice, and to stress the fact that where sin is uncovered, it is the sin—not the church—that summons sinners to conversion.

Finally, the allusion to collective sinfulness might arouse the same kinds of resistance that prompted the Israelite prophets to begin educating their people about personal responsibility. The important thing here is to differentiate distortion in the relationship to God from the issue of personal responsibility. What happened in history is what is being subjected to analysis, not the hearts of human beings; they are known only to God. Even canonized saints made mistakes.

Defined in the above terms, the concept of sin must be yoked with the concept of conversion. When the sinfulness of the world is laid bare, we cannot escape the issue of conversion. Our relationship to God must be made right. The effects of the way the world is now organized prove that it is a sinful world. Hence, if our relationship to God is to be authentic, we are obliged to participate somehow in transforming that world. Prayer is one form of involvement in that process.

Thus action for development, for structural transformation, for conscientization is an integral part of the way that leads to God. It verifies conversion. Such action has its own intrinsic meaning and import, of course—it envisions the well-being of humankind—but it is also an integral part of our relationship to God in Jesus Christ.

If the present structuring of the world is sinful, we cannot defend it, compromise with it, or resign ourselves to it, *and* claim at the same time that we are serving God. God does not want worship that obscures or minimizes urgent human needs. The sacrifice that pleases God is that of the heart whose penitence compels it to action. If the oppressed, upon hearing the good news of the kingdom of God, can stand up for their own liberation so that they may live in the image and likeness of God, then obviously the beneficiaries of their repression are called to conversion so that such liberation may be feasible. As I indicated in an earlier chapter, the needed reorganization of international relationships depends in large part on changing the assumptions that go unquestioned in the industrialized nations. I feel certain that theological examination and dissolution of those commonplace certitudes may be the only thing that will remove the obstacles to building a new international economic order.

At this juncture in history the church, with its own audience and means of interpretation, is compelled to say plainly what no one else dares to say—that is, that we must opt for the decision to change the world. For the church it is nothing less than a question of preaching the gospel message, whose function is to judge the world and thereby compel it to seek salvation. Needless to say, the church can do that only insofar as it is willing to submit to a critical analysis of its own history and practice. Once it has confessed its own sins, however, it will be in a position to lay bare the sinfulness of the world and to summon to conversion all those whose hearts are opened up by the exposé.

I readily admit that the church is not now disposed, prepared, or equipped to undertake that work of analysis. But the groundwork is being laid wherever church-affiliated activists are at work. They are helping to formulate this new message to a misshapen world, and we can already hear the basic strains in church pronouncements. In 1971, for example, the Pontifical Justice and Peace Commision offered the following observation for reflection by the Synod of Bishops:

> At the very heart of this world the church is to be the locus of conversion . . . the place where the reality of this world is revealed, where its injustice is laid bare . . . where all are summoned to conversion from this sinful world, not by fleeing the world but by participating in its transformation.

That point dovetails with a growing awareness in some sectors of the church. Many activists became involved in development work because charity impelled them to enter into solidarity with the poor. Their action became political as they analyzed the mechanisms of underdevelopment and saw clearly the need for structural transformation. At the same time they discovered that this work of theirs was the touchstone of truth for their faith, the verification of their conversion to God in Jesus Christ.

This radical change in perspective bears witness to recent progress in our understanding of the faith, of which praxis is the keynote and source. Set in motion by the impulse of charity as faith in action, work for the transformation of the world becomes a pathway to authentic, faith-inspired acknowledgment and worship of God. No longer is it just a basic dimension in *preaching* the gospel message. Now it is a basic requirement for *hearing* the word of God and *putting it into practice.* If resistance to injustice is stirred up whenever the presence of God is revealed, then God cannot be known or acknowledged by those who do not participate in changing practices and structures that entail injustice.

Thus the clearly defined notions of "sinful world" and "conversion" should dynamize those who believe in God; and they should provide an openness to God for those who want to change the world. I hope I have clarified their relevance for the tasks at hand.

Once the situation has been made clear, the mobilization of believers will depend on their good will, their generosity, and their boldness of spirit. But the task of theoretical elucidation remains basic to any mobilization process, and the church is capable of undertaking that task. Theoretical work is just as important as is the call to action. Indeed it arises out of ecclesial praxis and the questions raised by that praxis. The roles proposed for the church can be carried out only if the church is willing and able to explain satisfactorily how its actions are indeed a praxis of the faith.

Thesis 29: When individuals and nations free themselves from bondage, they discover that God is their liberator and creator summoning them to fashion their lives in the divine image and likeness.

When the organization of societal relationships not only fails to run smoothly but is seen as being in contradiction with God's design, those who suffered in resignation and despair begin to realize that they can liberate themselves from it. They are joined by those who have come to share their aspirations. Once they get a hold on reality, their movement toward liberation begins. Now nothing can stop them: "Shall tribulation, or distress, or persecution, or famine, or nakedness, or peril, or sword? . . . No . . . neither death, nor life, nor angels, nor principalities, nor things present, nor things to come, nor powers, nor height, nor depth, nor anything else in all creation" (Rom. 8:35–38). Such a step may take centuries, but it is irresistable once it becomes conceivable.

The signs of it are clear at this turning point in history. The various peoples of the earth have a long memory, and their patience is like an underground stream—potent though unseen. Those who dominate them barely suspect the frailty of their own authority, and they look ridiculous when they are caught up in a storm. Then those who have eyes to see know that their rulers are not deities or divine surrogates. If rulers are not truly the representatives of the people, they will keep their position only so long as the people puts up with them. They tremble on their thrones as surely as majestic trees do in a severe windstorm.

It is no accident that God's presence is revealed in the collapse of empires as well as in the passing breeze. God is present where human beings work for peace, and where they topple tyrants. God may love the "tranquility of order," but the divine presence is also manifested in the suppressed impatience that finally explodes amid entrenched disorder. Mary's Magnificat is radically subversive: it gives voice to centuries of impatience and hope.

The liberation movements set in motion by peoples when they can no longer put up with domination are like tidal waves. We glimpse something of the divine essence in their impulse for life, which is stronger than death. To be sure, we must do everything we can to avoid the excesses of such movements: we know the ravages they can cause. The violence of insurrection can be more destructive than the institutionalized violence it challenges. But the institutional violence may be so intense that insurrection becomes ineluctable. Such is the case when nothing is being done to effectively negotiate contradictions that have become intolerable.

It is at the extreme of insurrection that persons experience the liberation wherein God is revealed as their liberator. It is in the certitude of their liberation that some Christians are today recovering their memory. Rereading the Bible in the spirit in which it was written, they are reconstructing a concept of liberation that enables them to rediscover God in the very thrust of their own liberation.

Far from reducing faith to an ideology of revolution, the various liberation theologies spawned by the new impulse clearly represent our last chance to maintain control over the revolutions that are needed and to replace armed violence with the violence of debate. It is understandable that the church might be afraid of revolutions: their hostility to it caused it great suffering in the past.

Nevertheless the church has the heavy responsibility of making justified revolutions feasible at "the lowest human cost," as Father Lebret liked to put it. How is the church to do this? By examining revolutions in theological terms; by making clear to the world's peoples that God, who is also revealed in popular uprisings, is summoning them to keep their liberation movements under control and to regulate their impatience when they gain power. When violence is kept under control and mastered, it is far more liberating than unrestrained violence and the terror it unleashes.

For the first time in its history Christianity is being challenged to render conceivable a bloodless revolution. Within the framework of its own dynamism it is being asked to spell out the terms of a liberation process that will lead to the conversion of those who, perhaps without realizing it, have helped to solidify the societal structures responsible for dependence and underdevelopment.

Read from God's standpoint, sacred history points to God as the source of a people's liberation. Read from the viewpoint of a given people, sacred history makes clear that it will discover God as its liberator in the process of liberating itself. The two readings are complementary, not contradictory. They converge to form the concept of liberation underlying the language of revelation, which speaks of salvation and redemption.

Something very important and serious is at stake in the elaboration of liberation theologies. We cannot allow it to be undermined by ideological resistance to "bold innovations that will work profound changes" (*Populorum Progressio*, n. 32). Nor can we allow it to be slighted by reductionist efforts to turn the faith into nothing more than an ideology of revolution. At stake is the construction of a language that will make possible a divine message, a word of God. It may well be that only that message will enable us to gain appropriate mastery over the revolutions that must take place.

The fact is that the day of explosive revolutions is over. The transformations needed today are so broad-ranging and complex that only revolution by negotiation can succeed. I am not talking about "reformism," but about the responsible management of a new kind of revolution. Socio-political analysis enables us to ponder social dynamisms and envision our relative mastery over them. Theology has its role to play in elaborating the theory behind such an undertaking; it is already carrying out that role, thanks to Third World theologians. Instead of letting themselves be carried away by the intoxication of power, those theologians are rooting themselves deeper and deeper in their faith in God, a God who comes to life where human beings stand on their own two feet. Those theologians serve the revolution and give it a chance to be truly liberative simply by their being theologians, by having nothing to say except the word of God.

The resistance put up by various forms of dogmatism will undoubtedly discourage some of them. But the movement is so broad and powerful that God will be made known in the mighty wave that carries the real men and women of God and makes them speak. Their responsibility is great. Even greater is the responsibility of the church. They may fear the church, but only the church may be able to heed them and help them to maintain control over the power of their message and its potential effects.

It is a form of energy that is being liberated. Like nuclear energy, it can be destructive or liberative. The task at hand is to create another world—not a dreamland utopia but a concrete world in which human and international relationships are brought more in line with the demands of justice and fellowship. Step by step we must fashion a societal system that provides for a more equitable distribution of resources, production activities, and power, and gives freer rein to creative imagination. Together we must choose to undertake a praxis aimed at shaping a habitable world. We cannot alibi our way out by indulging in dreams of a perfect society or expatiating on the impotence of humanity to take charge of its history.

Shaping a habitable world is the vocation given to humanity when God is seen to be the creator of all things, and humanity is seen to be a creation made to the image and likeness of God. God is not the guardian of an order that has room only for passive submission. As the supreme creator, God offers us the vision of a creation to be completed and brought to fulfilment.

God makes clear to human beings what their own experience reveals to them—namely, that humanity exists only insofar as it fashions itself from its environment and organizes the world. A demiurge by vocation rather than by Promethean exhilaration, humanity must organize the world in line with its basic, constituent orientation. Obliged to build humanity from the data of nature and the collective memory of a humanization process that goes back millions of years, Adam and Eve now find themselves before a new threshold in the self-making process. From simply gathering available goods, they must move on to the organization and management of a patrimony that they now know is not inexhaustible. Leaving the "earthly paradise" where everything was handed to them, they must now organize their space and labor to produce the goods and services they need for survival. Beyond the ongoing task of mastering nature, which always remains a relative achievement, they must now maintain control over the organizations they need to set up for themselves and voluntarily choose to give direction to their history. That is the task to which they are summoned when God is revealed to them as their creator.

Creativity, as divine revelation confirms, is an essential constituent of human nature. It has nothing to do with megalomania. It is a thankless but necessary task: as thankless as that of Sisyphus, as necessary as that of earning a living.

God speaks to us about the liberation of captive energies and the creation of a world. The perspectives opened up to us by these two concepts are both exalting and compelling. We cannot operate with them irresponsibly: they are "dangerous"; but humanity fashions itself only by gauging and mastering the risks it must take.

Needless to say, these two concepts must be linked up with other concepts to become operative. Those other concepts come from other lines of thought that are part of the Judeo-Christian tradition, but their importance is more clearly seen in other traditions. These concepts focus on the "passivity" that structures the human effort just as much as "activity" does. Surrender to destiny or God is forced on every human being at one point or another—at the point of death if nowhere else. There can be no question of eliminating this "final vocation," but neither can we use it as an excuse for disregarding the task of societal creation.

The function of mystics is to keep humanity alert to our passage through death; but that function operates amid the more risky tasks of liberation and creation. Our second or final vocation is to find self-fulfilment in God through death. Only attention to that final vocation will enable us to confront the formidable demands of liberation and creativity in a serene and responsible way. Only if we conquer the fear of death will we be able to maintain mastery over the energies unleashed by liberation and their explosive potential.

God has something to say to every human being at this critical juncture. The role of the church is to let God speak by fashioning a language that can serve as the vehicle of the divine word.

Thesis 30: The earth has been entrusted to humanity—the unique collective subject of its history—and the goods of the earth are destined for all.

This perspective may seem unreal and utopian. But the creation of a world in which life is possible for all is a task that can be accomplished only by humanity as a whole. It is a collective task to be undertaken by humanity as one body, a unity yet to be composed. Never before in its history has humankind been called together in this way to function as a single body, to confront a challenge that can be met only in unison.

The myths of the tower of Babel and Prometheus in chains suggest that such an effort will run up against the taboos of one or more deity intent on retaining its monopoly of power and glory. The required collective effort is allegedly bound to end up in the collectivism of the anthill. Only aware and organized minorities can lead humanity along the right road, it is claimed, and they are likely to impose new forms of domination on everyone else. In short, there is every reason for humanity to stop, inhibited or paralyzed, before the obstacle that must be overcome. Icarus knows that his wings are in danger of being melted away if he flies too near the sun.

Christians may be more hesitant than others when faced with this demiurgic task. They are convinced that it represents a challenge even to God. More than others, then, they must realize that it is precisely God who is summoning them to fashion a world in which life is possible for all.

The second creation account in the Book of Genesis (2:5-25) depicts the origination of the human race in the form of a single human being. Before any mention of male and female, God creates Adam as a single, unique subject, called to a life in the divine image and likeness. The radical oneness of humanity is thus singled out as something prior to the personal destiny that individuals fashion in and out of a group life. The transcendence involved in personalization does not entail an uprooting from the aboriginal unity. This archaic truth remains the underlying infrastructure of the humanization process that accompanies any and every form of true human progress. The experience accumulated in the collective memory ever remains the source of all self-creation. Human origination, evoked in religious myth at such a deep level that it appears to be a structure, denotes rather a horizon and a projection.

Near the end of Judeo-Christian scriptural revelation Paul expresses the same truth clearly when he talks about Christ, the new Adam in whom all are gathered together once again: "You are all one in Christ Jesus." Writing in Greek, he could have used the neuter *hen* for "one," thus giving this statement the ambiguity of a symbol. Instead he employs the masculine form *heis*, as if to make clear that he is talking about a single human subject, a single offspring of

God: "Neither Jew nor Greek . . . neither slave nor free . . . neither male nor female . . ." (Gal. 3:28). What myth had said in its way, Paul says clearly in talking about the one in whom he sees all being "recapitulated." In God's eyes all are "as one single human," whose vocation is to be the child of God, wholly like the Father, in the Spirit. Paul points to a vocation that transcends history yet gives history its meaning.

It is this unique progeny of God that is summoned to be the collective subject and agent of its own history. To it is entrusted the earth, to be managed and made habitable.

That the goods of the earth are destined for all is taught in this revelation. It is not just an ethical principle or postulate. It is a vocation and a task that must be carried out if the earth is really to belong to all. Here is the source and foundation of the efforts considered in a previous chapter to resist societal inequality—that is, those of the Israelite lawgivers, the prophets, Jesus, and the church fathers. Created in the image and likeness of God, Adam (man and woman, every human group, humanity) is here set before the real task: not to build a tower in defiance of God, but to manage a patrimony so that all may have an opportunity for self-creation and ascent to God.

Deep-rooted as our certainty about this issue may be, it remains a task to be undertaken rather than a glorious achievement to be contemplated. Avoiding narcissism and megalomania, humanity must work to set history on the path indicated.

The church fathers were willing to pursue the implications of this vocation to the very end. Inasmuch as the goods of the earth are destined for all, they said, those in extreme necessity have the right to take what they desperately need wherever they may find it. It was a deeply subversive statement, and little was done to implement it for centuries. Yet it never wholly disappeared from the collective memory, and today it has resurfaced as a clear and obvious principle:

> All other rights, whatever they may be, including the rights of property ownership and free trade, are to be subordinated to this principle. They should in no way hinder it; in fact, they should actively facilitate its implementation. Redirecting these rights back to their original purpose must be regarded as an important and urgent social duty [Paul. VI, *Populorum Progressio*, n. 22].

However, there is no point in reaffirming such a right if we do not spell out the conditions involved in making it a reality. Simply to reiterate the conclusion of the church fathers is to say little or nothing. The inequitable distribution of goods is now a fact on a worldwide scale, but those dying of hunger cannot take what they need. The goods are "elsewhere," and they have no access to them. If the word of God is not to be reduced to empty verbiage, a responsible theological effort is needed to spell out the conditions surrounding its implementation. Here representatives of the Third World have provided theologians with the "mediation" they needed to make the word of God speak—namely, by posing the issue of the construction of a new international economic order.

If the earth truly is meant to provide all with the goods they need, then it must be organized accordingly. Humanity cannot refuse this task if it wants to keep moving forward rather than slip back into barbarism. Amid the web of conflicting interests and contradictions, which cannot be solved by merely reversing the present set of power balances, humanity is beginning to see that this task is what constitutes its unity. Alterations in relationships of power will enable it to envision ways to negotiate potential relationships of complementarity.

To speak of negotiation in a cultural setting structured around the awareness of conflict and class struggle is to risk being disparagingly labeled an advocate of reformism or some silly "third way" approach. The question is so serious, however, that I choose to run that risk.

Societies structure themselves by continually negotiating their contradictions. They reach an impasse when those contradictions harden in the infrastructure and the collective consciousness, and thus make negotiation impossible. And it is obvious that the nascent global society, the only framework in which societal dynamics are now intelligible and manageable, can be built up only through negotiation. There is no world authority to implement such a project by imposition. Indeed it is almost impossible to envision the imposition and acceptance of global domination, though that hypothesis cannot be utterly ruled out if negotiation fails.

The Third World has called for such negotiation to achieve a new international economic order. It is a summons to all humankind, urging it to take charge of the course of its history. If that negotiation is slow in coming, it is because it is almost inconceivable and because it means a break with the sacrosanct principles of liberalism, free trade, the law of supply and demand, comparative advantages, and so forth.

Humanity must be provided with every means that will make such negotiation conceivable. In its language, derived from its praxis, Christianity does have concepts to offer: the oneness of the human race, and the conviction that the goods of this earth are destined for all. Once brought together, they will make it possible for persons to see negotiation as an urgent and obligatory task. As a historical movement capable of self-interpretation, Christianity should once again take up the task of elaborating those two concepts and presenting them to the world, so that humankind may see its collective task more clearly and then take it in hand.

The church understandably hesitates to assume such a role. In the light of its past history, its intervention in worldly affairs may be dreaded; and it still feels the sting of criticism leveled at its intervention in the past. Nevertheless this mutual apprehension must be surmounted. The church must put to use its talents received as a deposit in trust. It must do so in order to be faithful to its tradition. If it is to have something to say to a listening world, it must utter the message that wells up from its original thrust: a subversive message vis-à-vis established disorder.

If the church decides to do this, it must speak with the humility of a servant who has not always played its proper role in the service of truth. A laying down of norms is not what the world is expecting from the church, though many church officials think otherwise. The world simply wants to be assured that the church does have some guideposts for the road that must be mapped out.

The objective, the collective task we face, is a global order that will ensure that the needs of all can be satisfied. As the political will to undertake that task becomes a reality, the two concepts furnished by the church will enable us to define the collective subject of that task and the goal that should inspire it.

However, there is no ready-made model of the order we are seeking to construct. That must be worked out in the process of negotiation, with all interested parties involved. But a basic orientation and direction is clear. We can envision the task that must be carried out, even though it yet remains to be done.

Christianity helped to legitimate a world order that sacralized territorial delimitations and property ownership. The church will recover its foundational identity and dynamism to the extent that it delivers a message subversive of that order. The relevance of the word of God to the contemporary world hinges on its relevance to the inescapable tasks confronting humankind. Those who deny or ignore God may or may not have their denial or their ignorance shattered by God. That, we may say, is "God's business." The business of the church is to broadcast the word that God speaks to it.

Chapter 8

Political and Theological Praxis of the Faith

As the conditions of the church's historical existence are brought out, the church itself is led to a faith-practice entailing primarily the conscientization of human groups and the education of public opinion. The aim in view is for humanity to take voluntary charge of its history, as it now must.

Political involvement in history does not turn the church away from God by any means. Indeed it enables the church to rediscover God; and specifically, to rediscover God's radical demand that justice be turned into a reality. Theological work is needed to establish the link between recognition of God and the construction of human societies. That theological task, however, must now become the task of the whole church.

Thesis 31: In the role the church has to play in the transformation of the world, it must take into account the political consequences of preaching the gospel.

When God's presence is revealed, it changes the world. Those who heed God cannot possibly be a party to organized societal relationships that necessarily entail underdevelopment, injustice, and poverty for most of humanity. As the liberator of peoples, God summons them to build a society structured so as to satisfy the basic needs of all: goods, services, security, peace, and happiness.

To believe in God, therefore, does not mean to withdraw from the world in order to contemplate God—unless one has received the specific vocation to bear that sort of witness to God's active presence in a world that has forgotten God. Believing in God means setting to work to create a world in which every human being can find self-fulfilment in God's image and likeness. Thus analysis of underdevelopment and of the prerequisites for generalized development, and study of the history, memory, and language of the Judeo-Christian tradition, inevitably end up in a political praxis of the faith.

I mentioned earlier that church activists and officials had become involved in the needs of the poor around the world out of a sense of charity and their obligations. Then they gradually came to see that existing structures had to be transformed, and that involvement in this obviously political task was imposed on them by faith itself. This is one of the most astonishing and radical shifts in

102

perspective ever witnessed in church history: from charity spurring believers to engage in political activity, to a political praxis that serves to point up and verify the exigencies of authentic faith. So astonishing is this shift that the church had to do violence to itself in order to accept it and live it. For several centuries it had been in the process of freeing itself from its entanglements in the politics of Christendom, from its role as the guardian of the civil religon of the West. As this process of depoliticization reached its climax, the church suddenly found itself compelled to deal with the inevitable political consequences of preaching the gospel message as something incarnate in history, as something relevant, operative, and effective.

Not surprisingly, such a reversal met with resistance in a cultural milieu that took it for granted that politics was in the process of becoming secularized, rational, and scientific. This assumption, of course, helped to conceal the proliferation of new false gods, some of which appealed to the God of Jesus Christ for support. In such a situation the church could not shirk its responsibilities: its witness to divine salvation never ceases to entail the profanation of idols.

The new political practice of the faith, now incumbent on the church, can have no other aim than the construction of a world in which every human being has a chance to achieve full humanity. It is not a matter of debating ideas, if indulging in ideological confrontations that end up as religious wars. What is involved here is a practice aimed at building a world society, because no society is any longer possible otherwise. That practice must tackle the causes of the present situation. The effects are already well known to us from structural analysis: human beings are dying of starvation and hopelessness; they have little or no chance to live a decent life.

To get beyond the debating of ideas, however, we must do something about the group certitudes and mental structures that permit the present organization of the world to persist as if it were the most natural thing in the world. We must work on ideas and educate public opinion in order to foster the political will needed to change the world. This work is an authentic and essential part of the political practice I am discussing here. It is needed to develop the power or counterpower we must have in order to bring about change, in order to compel humanity to organize the kind of society required to deal with the tasks facing us.

This revolution, so badly needed, is a new kind of revolution. No past revolution serves as an appropriate model. The revolutions of an earlier day have exhausted their capacity to furnish the relationships now required for the societal organization of humanity. Their palpable effects continue in existence, however, obstructing the pathways we must now open up and explore. The entire undertaking remains to be done, though we may find some of the groundwork laid in certain socialist revolutions and some attempts at negotiation.

Those who have the function of pondering what roads we are to take in the future bear a heavy responsibility. They must try to clear the brush and open up as yet unexplored paths. They must be critical in order to be constructive and forward-looking. Even more than others, they must be wary of bowing to ready-made ideas. From experience they know that research begins with doubt, with calling into question stereotyped certitudes that are no longer functional.

Theologians are called upon to act as poets, artists, and prophets. They are summoned to ponder a new future for humanity, knowing full well that God wants humanity to be in the divine image and likeness, creative of the conditions needed for true communion.

Such is the political practice of the faith that the people of God is called to exercise. It has nothing to do with being carried away by some religious ideology and losing oneself in the world. Rather, it is in the very logic of the mystery of the Incarnation. We must speak God where God speaks—there where human beings try to stand on their own feet and build their way to God. Down through the ages they search for God, organizing and working to find their place in the sun. In the midst of a nature that produces everything except human existence, humanity comes to exist only insofar as it transforms nature in accordance with its own basic teleology.

This new political praxis of the faith has nothing to do with the clerical politics of the past. It is not aimed at implementing a "political program derived from the very words of sacred scripture." Instead its aim is to liberate the dynamics of societal life and to enhance the ability of human beings to control those dynamisms. It has nothing to do with imposing a model allegedly of divine inspiration. Its aim is to ensure that human beings and societies regain self-determination over their collective life.

The main obstacle to true human progress may well be ideological: social "scientism," traces of which can be found both in a certain social doctrine of the church and in a certain Marxism. This social scientism would grant power only to those who know—that is, think they know—how societies should be fashioned. The masses would merely pay the expenses for these demiurges, whose cynicism is often concealed under their illusions of knowledge.

Authentic political leaders are those who do not know, and who therefore go looking for the best possible procedures and alternatives in a given situation. They are courageous enough to have doubts, to question themselves, to ponder the course of action to which they must commit those who have delegated authority to them.

The growing doubts in our collective awareness about the present global system are eating away at the smugness of those who think they know everything, who seem to learn nothing from their repeated failures. It is an opportune moment for a new political practice based, not on prefabricated ideas, but on a willingness to raise the real questions on which the future of humanity depends.

In such a context our political practice of the faith will have to be "prophetic." I do not mean we shall be diviners of the future. I mean we shall be like stargazers peering into the darkness to make out the signs of the time, to see what is necessary and what is possible.

There can be no doubt that the role of believers is to work at making such a political practice possible. There can be no doubt that the church, which did so much to substitute ideology for practice, must now try to make such a politics conceivable and feasible. Human beings, it seems, mobilize as a group only when someone gets them to dream dreams. Then comes the rude awakening. Right now the disenchantment may be bad enough to jolt those who are beginning to realize that they really do not know what the story is, to open their eyes to the thankless but necessary tasks on which our future depends.

The theoretical task incumbent on the church right now is one of its most important tasks, if the church is to do its part at this critical juncture in history. That task must be carried out if the church is to give a proof of the truth and relevance of the faith it proclaims and practices.

Thesis 32: God alone is God.

God is wholly different from everything else that exists, thereby liberating humanity and entrusting it with authority and a mission vis-à-vis the rest of creation.

To say that God is wholly other is to make clear that God is always above and beyond any representations of God that we might conceive. God *is,* as inconceivable as nothingness. But because God exists, God stands on the horizon of everything that human beings have said ever since they began to speak. God's presence-in-absence structures and opens human consciousness so that it can never again close in upon itself definitively, or confine itself to a world that it has definitively apprehended and mastered. God's transcendence grounds the transcendence of the human being, who must keep opening out to others and to God. As humankind collectively fashions itself, every human being has a chance to develop a personal existence out of the collected store of human experience and genetic inheritance.

In our day persons have come to pose the question of God's existence as if God could be situated somewhere "out there" like any other object. Hence it must be made clear that a god that is not above and beyond all representation and all questioning is not God. God is present by virtue of everything that is not God, structuring our representation of everything that exists.

God the unknowable is made known only in the experience of those who speak in God's name, of those whose lives tell others what sovereign freedom is. Jesus of Nazareth is eminently one of those persons. Profaning Caesar and slighting the law, Jesus summons all his listeners to find self-fulfilment in his fulness as the Son of God. He does not call them to indulge in idle dreams or to evade their thankless but obligatory tasks. Instead he summons them to face death at the end of the road, upon completion of the task that every human is called to perform. Jesus frees the energy needed to confront that other enemy to human progress: inertia. Like all life, the collective life of humanity is an ongoing battle against crystalization: against the tendency of societies to structure themselves in terms of inequality.

If God alone is God, then everything else is a task to be accomplished, a task to be picked up again and again from the very beginning. The accumulation of experiences and memories is merely the starting point for imagination, innovation, and creation, on which life depends.

Functioning societies sacralize their structures so that they may function better. When those structures do not function, we must be able to desacralize them. In the rush of scientific discoveries and rational progress over the past few centuries, some came to believe that the negation of God, methodological or existential, was necessary if human beings were going to build the world and take charge of their history. Now the moment has come when God must again come to the aid of a humanity that has begun to have doubts about its creative capacities. Supreme creator, God confirms the necessity of the collective human task and the need for humanity to create itself by shaping the world. And only God can provide that confirmation.

In the final instance, some human beings may be called to "lose" themselves in God. But humankind is first placed in the world by God to collectively carry out a task it cannot evade. It is God who plunges humanity into the affairs of this world and entrusts it with a creative function. Far from being the fanciful projection of impotent dreams, God is the one who calls humanity into existence and gives it a world to build.

The realization that God alone is God opens up a broad field of action for humanity. No mastery is ruled out once its necessity becomes evident. God is not the guardian of any natural or divine order that is to be left untouched. God's presence-in-absence removes all the taboos with which human beings surround themselves to delimit the realm of the feared unknown. Reducing the stars to landmarks and Caesar to a tax collector, God opens out the field of human endeavor to infinity. Setting aside Christendom's use of God in an earlier day, and the negation of God in modern times, we must now try to encounter God frontally, without preconceived notions. Only then shall we have the courage and audacity to build a new kind of society, one of which God will not be the pillar and support, because we shall finally have come to realize that society is the work of human hands: precarious, provisional, and in need of constant reworking.

Because God is present by total absence, the human race finds itself facing the task at hand alone. And that task, we are now beginning to realize, is a matter of life and death. When rulers could claim to be gods or the envoys of God, it was easy enough to get whole people to trust them and pay the costs of lavish palaces and tombs. Even the denial of God helped rulers to turn the religious impulses of a people to their own advantage. Once God begins to be truly God, however, the tax collectors must account for their exercise of delegated authority. Revelation of the true God means the profanation of all earthly things, and politics is restored to its proper dimensions. Once the involvement of religion in politics can be overcome, then religious practice can use the search for God as the measure of its authenticity. Divine worship can no longer serve as an alibi for human inertia. Instead it can serve to point to the transcendence of life in all progressive achievements and the altruism that is released when society shapes its own existence—or better, when the conditions theoretically necessary for self-creation are finally in place, because society will never cease creating itself as long as there are human beings. The "end of history" is a myth that we must free ourselves from if we are not to remain enslaved to visionary tomorrows. Experience has proved that messianisms, too, can end up in terror.

God makes human beings free—or God is not God. Those who have caught a glimpse of the true God no longer fear power and authority, no longer fear death, though they realize that their conquest of fear must begin over again every day. Empires begin to totter when such persons grow in number. Repression may crush them one by one, but they rise from their ashes. The poor, the lowly who believe in God, are those who now make it possible for us to envision the worldwide revolution needed by us all. The good news proclaimed to them enables them to be born to freedom. They can die because they have already conquered death.

Christianity no longer has to try to force itself on anyone, thus running the risk of turning into a civil religion. It can once again play its proper role in history, bearing witness to the presence of the God whose absence ensures history's fulfilment. Eliminating the last vestiges of the older social and mental structures that it helped to shape and sacralize, it can now strip down to the basic dynamics of faith and the minimum of language and structure needed for its collective existence. It can once again become the liberation movement it was at the start.

"Losing oneself in God" will again be possible, even for those who are absorbed with secular preoccupations. At the close of busy, work-filled days God will be present for the refreshment of their spirits. They will be able to chant the glory of God even before they have finished their work completely.

As for those who claim to believe in God and use God to conserve the present "order," they will gradually fade into the background. It will become increasingly obvious that God could never stoop to the functions they take for granted. Reared by a church that believed God had entrusted the government of the world to it, they may still find conversion in a church that has turned back to the God of Jesus Christ. We may hope that they, too, will die to their dreams of power and be reborn to the life and liberty of God's children.

God alone is God. Life becomes possible once again. And there will be no lack of work for those who are willing to participate in what must be done. Having rejected the dreamers and princes of this world, a people on the march will recover its memory and extract from it the ideas and procedures it needs to achieve self-determination.

God alone is God. Human beings are free.

Thesis 33: The role of theology is to render an account of the praxis of the faith.

Once it has decided to assume its proper role, the church discovers as it goes along that it has kept the memory of practices that tie in with what it must do today. In its memory it finds concepts that enable it to ponder what it must do in accordance with what it truly is. The church is called back to its true origin and identity. It must die to power in order to be reborn in all its nakedness.

We must have a correct understanding of the theological work to be undertaken in connection with this venture. It is not a matter of going back to some perduring foundational theory in order to elaborate another theory that will tell us what we must do. Prior to any and all theory is practice. The divine word spoken in the church is the only word that dares to call itself creative, that dares to become incarnate. It does what it says, even before it is spoken. God creates the world in order to utter the word that creates it. The people of God and all peoples engage in a process of self-liberation, thus becoming free to say that God is their liberator. It is because human beings act in the world that they speak of God. They do not invoke God just to speak of what they cannot do, or to have God speak of the deeds they can only dream of doing.

The anteriority of practice to theory opens to theology a field of work from which it should never have departed to indulge in elaborations claiming to tell us what ought to be done. Theological reasoning can be normative only in the sense that the explanation of a craftsman can be normative: telling us how something should be done because experience shows it is the best or only way to do it. The validity of such an explanation is verified by practice.

God's revelation in history takes place in and through a praxis of liberation that includes resisting structural injustice and desacralizing everything that is not God. Everything uttered in the word of God finds its starting point in the pursuits of human beings, who look for God as they go about their earthly tasks and make history. It is that history itself that is revelatory. Interpreted as it takes shape, it speaks of God.

Knowing that the word of God is formulated only in the words of human beings speaking about God, we can explore it endlessly without ever exhausting what it has to say. It is merely a path to the silence in which God speaks the divine essence. Although scriptural revelation closed with the death of the last apostle, the word of God is not fixed in any text or discourse that might serve as the norm of norms. Its interpretation springs from the same process that brings it into being. In short, it derives from practice.

The liberation of theology is undoubtedly the task on which hinges our assumption of all other tasks. It can be carried out only in the course of its practice. To theorize about it before we start would be to doom the enterprise to misunderstanding and incomprehension. Interpretation of the word of God must follow the same course as the formulation of that word, if we are to prove its relevance and efficacy. Reasoning itself is worth little more than straw, as Thomas Aquinas realized. What matters is the practice that it makes feasible, a practice aimed at changing the world.

Changing the world is what counts, and we must free ourselves from the fetters that make that task impossible. God is not in those fetters. Indeed it is God who liberates believers and sends them out into the vineyard where "the last shall be first."

Like the laborers of the eleventh hour, theologians may well be the last to get there. Workers are already in the field, fashioning bit by bit the conditions for an authentic human existence for all. They are the ones entrusted with that task, and some of them seek and find God in their work. The role of theologians is to pay heed to that praxis and construct the language that those who are doing it need to express what they are experiencing in it.

Although they may be the last to get to the vineyard, theologians can be the first to celebrate the festivities. Their function, in fact, is to pave the way for the celebration of God's glory embodied in a humanity living the life of God. The role is similar to that of the wandering minstrel in West Africa who is supposed to take charge of festivals and create the proper ambiance and enthusiasm for the hard work that must follow.

Having seen the ravages of an ethereal theology that turned human beings away from their earthly tasks, we can only hope that theologians will be the last to prevent persons from standing on their own two feet and building a world in which they can hymn the glory of God. Wise theologians have always known that God speaks when they shut up and let God do God's work, when they demolish false representations of God and help human beings to turn their history into a history of Emmanuel—God with us.

This theological effort to rediscover the dynamic thrust of sacred history is just as important as the committed involvement of Christians and the church in the transformation of the world. A century of critical exegesis and hermeneutics has laid the groundwork needed to carry out the task. Now theology must try to

for believers to comprehend the pris-
of living in God's image and like-

emory. It will be prophetic and
nd contemplates the work of God in
for all humankind. That type of
se who are trying to render an ac-
a praxis in history.